How Elections Work
IN PLAIN ENGLISH

A Guide For The Everyday Voter

By Brian C Eby

Table of Contents

Chapter 1

Introduction

In the United States, voting is both a right and a responsibility—a cornerstone of democracy that has evolved through centuries of struggle, reform, and participation. From the earliest days of the republic, when only a select few could cast their ballots, to the present day, when millions of voices come together to shape the nation's future, voting has always been more than just a civic duty. It is a profound expression of freedom, a testament to the power of the people to determine their destiny.

But for many, the intricacies of the US voting system remain shrouded in complexity and confusion. With each election cycle, questions arise: How does the Electoral College work? Why do some states hold caucuses while others have primaries? What exactly is a superdelegate, and how do they influence the outcome of a nomination? These questions are not merely academic—they strike at the heart of how democracy functions in America.

The Purpose of This Book:

This book invites readers to delve into the mechanisms that drive the US voting process, explore its historical context, and understand the challenges and opportunities ahead. It guides citizens who wish to be informed participants in their democracy and exercise their right to vote confidently and clearly, empowering them with the knowledge to navigate the complexities of the US electoral system.

As we work through the labyrinth of American elections, we will uncover the forces that have shaped the voting process—from the early exclusionary practices that denied many the right to vote to the hard-fought victories that expanded suffrage to include women, people of color, and younger citizens. We will examine the role of technology in modern voting, the ongoing debates over election security, and the impact of third-party candidates in a predominantly two-party system.

Most importantly, this book seeks to empower you, the reader, with the knowledge to navigate the complexities of the US electoral system. Whether you are a first-time voter or a seasoned participant in the democratic process, understanding how elections work is crucial to ensuring your voice is heard.

Importance of Voting

In the following pages, we will break down each component of the voting process, from voter registration to the final counting of ballots. In the appendix, we will also provide a state-by-state guide, offering detailed information on how each state conducts its elections, the number of electoral votes it holds, and any unique characteristics that set it apart from the rest of the country.

Voting is not just about selecting leaders; it is about participating in the ongoing experiment of American democracy. It is a reminder that the power to shape the future lies in the hands of the people. As you read this book, may you find answers to your questions and inspiration to participate in this great democratic tradition, reinforcing the importance of your role in the US voting process.

Chapter 2

The Structure of the US Voting System

Federal vs State Control:

The United States is a nation built on a unique balance of power between the federal government and individual states. This balance is nowhere more evident than in the administration of elections. While the Constitution grants the federal government the authority to regulate certain aspects of elections, it also gives states significant autonomy in managing their electoral processes. This dual system has shaped how Americans vote, leading to a nationwide patchwork of voting practices.

The Federal Role in Elections

The federal government's involvement in elections is primarily rooted in the Constitution. Key amendments, such as the 15th, 19th, and 26th

Amendments, have expanded suffrage and prohibited discrimination based on race, gender, and age. Additionally, the federal government plays a crucial role in regulating campaign finance, setting the date for federal elections, and ensuring the protection of voters' rights through legislation such as the Voting Rights Act of 1965.

One of the most significant ways the federal government influences elections is by regulating the Electoral College, which ultimately elects the President and Vice President. Established by the Constitution, this system balances the influence of populous and less populous states. The federal government sets the number of electoral votes each state receives based on its congressional representation, directly affecting presidential election outcomes.

Furthermore, the Help America Vote Act (HAVA) of 2002 is another example of federal legislation shaping the voting landscape. Passed in response to the controversies of the 2000 presidential election, HAVA aimed to improve the administration of elections by setting minimum standards for states to follow, including the modernization of voting equipment and the creation of statewide voter registration databases.

The State's Role in Elections

Despite the federal government's overarching role, the day-to-day administration of elections falls mainly to the states. Each state has the authority to determine how elections are conducted, who is eligible to vote, and how votes are counted. This means that the specifics of voting—such as voter registration procedures, identification requirements, and the methods of voting available—can vary widely from state to state.

For instance, some states offer same-day voter registration, allowing citizens to register and vote on Election Day, while others require voters to register weeks or even months in advance. Similarly, states have different rules regarding voter identification; some require a government-issued photo ID, while others accept a broader range of identification or none.

States also have the authority to decide how they will manage their primary elections, whether through open or closed primaries or even caucuses, and these decisions can significantly influence the outcome of elections. Additionally, states can choose to implement early voting or no-excuse absentee voting, offering more flexibility to voters who cannot vote on Election Day.

The autonomy given to states allows for experimentation and innovation in elections. For example, Oregon, Washington, and Colorado have adopted universal vote-by-mail systems, where all registered voters receive their ballots by mail and can return them by mail or drop them off at designated locations. These systems have been praised for increasing voter turnout and reducing election costs.

The Balance of Power: Benefits and Challenges

The division of electoral authority between the federal and state governments has benefits. It allows for flexibility and innovation, as states can tailor their election procedures to suit their needs and demographics. This system also checks federal power, ensuring that states retain a significant role in one of the most fundamental aspects of democracy.

However, this balance of power also presents challenges. The variation in election laws and procedures across states can lead to confusion among voters, especially in an increasingly mobile society where people frequently move across state lines. Additionally, disparities in election administration can result in unequal access to the ballot box, with some voters facing more obstacles than others depending on where they live.

The lack of uniformity can also complicate efforts to ensure election security and integrity. While states are responsible for securing their election systems, the federal government is vested in protecting elections from interference and ensuring all citizens have equal access to vote. This has led to ongoing debates about the appropriate balance of power between the federal government and the states in administering elections.

The Future of Federal and State Control in Elections

As the US continues to grapple with issues of voter access, election security, and the fairness of the Electoral College, the balance of power between federal and state governments will remain a central issue. Ongoing debates about voting rights, gerrymandering, and the role of technology in elections are likely to shape future changes in how elections are conducted.

Understanding this balance of power is crucial for any voter. It underscores the importance of staying informed about federal and state election laws and how they affect one's right to vote. In a nation as diverse and complex as the United States, the interplay between federal oversight and state autonomy ensures that the voting process remains dynamic, evolving with the needs and values of the electorate.

Types of Elections:

Primaries, General Elections, and Special Elections

The United States operates a complex and multifaceted electoral system accommodating various elections. Understanding the different types of elections is vital to grasping how American democracy functions. In this section, we'll explore the primary types of elections: primaries, general elections, and special elections, each of which serves a distinct purpose in the political process.

Primaries are the first step in the electoral process for many political offices, especially for presidential and congressional races. These elections determine which candidates will represent their respective parties in the general election. There are several types of primary elections, each with rules and implications.

- **Closed Primaries:** In a closed primary, only registered members of a political party can vote to choose their party's candidate. For example, in a state with a closed primary system, a registered Democrat would only be allowed to vote in the Democratic primary and a registered Republican in the Republican primary.

This system ensures that only party members can select their party's nominee.

- **Open Primaries:** Unlike closed primaries, open primaries allow all registered voters to participate, regardless of their party affiliation. Voters in an open primary can choose which party's primary they want to vote in, but they can only vote in one. This system is often praised for being more inclusive, allowing independent voters or those not aligned with a major party to have a say in candidate selection.

- **Semi-Closed Primaries:** Some states use a semi-closed primary system, in which registered party members can only vote in their own party's primary, but independent voters can choose which primary to participate. This hybrid approach aims to balance inclusivity with the integrity of the party selection process.

- **Top-Two Primaries:** In this system, sometimes called a "jungle primary," all candidates compete in a single primary, regardless of party affiliation. The top two vote-getters, regardless of party, then move on to the general election. This system is used in states like California and Washington and is intended to produce more centrist candidates by forcing them to appeal to a broader electorate.

- **Caucuses:** While not a primary in the traditional sense, caucuses are another method of selecting party nominees. Instead of a straightforward voting process, caucuses involve local gatherings of party members who debate and vote on candidates in a more communal and public setting. States like Iowa and Nevada are well-known for their caucus systems, which favor candidates with strong grassroots support.

Whether open, closed, or otherwise, primaries are critical to the US electoral system. They serve as a testing ground for candidates, helping to winnow the field and allowing voters to directly impact who will represent their party in the general election.

General Elections: Deciding the Leaders

The general election is the main event in the US electoral process, where voters decide who will hold public office. General elections are held at regular intervals, most notably every four years for the President and every two years for members of Congress. These elections typically occur the first Tuesday after the first Monday in November.

- **Presidential Elections:** Presidential elections occur every four years and are perhaps the most closely watched events in American politics. Voters do not directly elect the President; instead, they vote for a slate of electors pledged to support a particular candidate in the Electoral College. The candidate who receives a majority of electoral votes wins the presidency. The structure and timing of presidential elections ensure that they dominate the political landscape, often overshadowing other races.

- **Congressional Elections:** Congressional elections include Senate and House of Representatives races. Senators serve six-year terms, with approximately one-third of the Senate up for election every two years. House members serve two-year terms, meaning all 435 seats are contested in every general election. These elections are crucial for determining the balance of power in Congress, which can significantly impact the legislative agenda for the next two years.

- **Gubernatorial and State Elections:** In addition to federal races, general elections often include gubernatorial and state legislative races. Governors serve as the chief executives of their states, and their elections can be hotly contested, especially in battleground states. State legislatures, which are responsible for passing state laws and budgets, also see their seats filled through general elections.

- **Local Elections:** Though they receive less attention, local elections are vital to the functioning of democracy. These elections determine who will hold office, such as mayor, city council, county commissioner, and school board members. Local elected officials directly impact citizens' day-to-day lives, making these elections just as crucial as those for higher office.

General elections are the culmination of the electoral process. Voters have the final say in who will represent them at various levels of government. The outcomes of these elections shape the direction of public policy and the nation's future.

Special Elections: Filling Vacancies and Deciding Urgent Issues

Special elections are held to fill vacancies between regular election cycles or address urgent matters that cannot wait until the next election. These elections can occur anytime and attract intense interest, particularly involving high-profile offices.

- **Filling Vacancies:** Special elections are commonly held when an officeholder resigns, passes away, or cannot continue serving. For example, if a US Senator steps down before the end of their term, a special election may be called to fill the seat until the next regular election. These elections are crucial because they can alter the balance of power, particularly in closely divided legislative bodies.

- **Ballot Measures and Referenda:** Special elections are also used to vote on specific issues, such as proposed laws, constitutional amendments, or local initiatives. These ballot measures can have significant consequences, often addressing matters of public policy that require immediate attention. For instance, a state might hold a special election to decide on a tax increase, a bond measure for infrastructure projects, or changes to voting laws.

- **Recall Elections:** In some states, voters can recall elected officials before their terms are up. If enough voters sign a petition, a recall election can be triggered, allowing the electorate to decide whether to remove the official from office. Recall elections are rare but can occur when widespread dissatisfaction with an officeholder's performance exists.

While less common than primaries and general elections, special elections play a critical role in maintaining the continuity of government and ensuring that urgent issues are addressed promptly. They also allow voters to influence government decisions outside the regular election schedule.

The Role of the Electoral College

The Electoral College is one of the U.S. electoral system's most distinctive and sometimes controversial elements. Unlike other elections in the United States, where candidates are elected directly by popular vote, the presidency is decided by this unique mechanism, which has its roots in the Constitution. Understanding the Electoral College is crucial to grasping how American presidential elections work.

The Basics of the Electoral College

The Electoral College is not a physical place but a process by which electors, chosen by the states, vote to elect the President and Vice President of the United States. The Constitution established the system as a compromise between those who wanted the President to be elected by Congress and those who favored election by a popular vote.

Each state is allocated several electors equal to the total number of its Senators and Representatives in Congress, with Washington, D.C., receiving three electors thanks to the 23rd Amendment. This brings the total number of electors to 538. A majority of 270 electoral votes is required to win the presidency.

How the Electoral College Works

On Election Day, when citizens vote for President, they vote for a slate of electors chosen by their party who are pledged to vote for that party's candidate. In 48 states and Washington, D.C., the candidate who wins the popular vote in that state takes all of its electoral votes—a system known as "winner-take-all." Maine and Nebraska use a proportional method, awarding electoral votes based on the popular vote in each congressional district and the statewide result.

After the general election, these electors meet in their respective states in December to vote for President and Vice President. These votes are then sent to Congress and officially counted in a joint session in January. The candidate who receives the majority of electoral votes is declared the winner.

Criticisms and Controversies

The Electoral College has faced significant criticism over the years, mainly because it can—and has—led to situations where a candidate wins the presidency despite losing the national popular vote. This occurred in five elections, most recently in 2000 and 2016. Critics argue that the Electoral College gives disproportionate power to smaller states and can lead to a focus on a few key "swing states" during campaigns, potentially neglecting voters in other regions.

Moreover, the system's origins are tied to historical compromises, including the Three-Fifths Compromise, which initially gave Southern slave states more influence. These issues have sparked ongoing and lively debates about the Electoral College's relevance in modern American democracy. As a concerned citizen, you might find yourself advocating for its abolition in favor of a national popular vote.

The Future of the Electoral College

Despite the criticisms, changing the Electoral College would require a challenging and complex constitutional amendment. Some states have explored alternatives, such as the National Popular Vote Interstate Compact, where states agree to allocate their electoral votes to the candidate who wins the national popular vote. Still, this compact has not yet been adopted by enough states to take effect.

Understanding the Electoral College is essential to understanding how U.S. presidential elections are conducted and why they sometimes yield results that differ from the popular vote. As debates about its future continue, the Electoral College remains a central feature of American democracy, with your voice and opinion being part of this ongoing discussion.

Electoral Votes Allocation: How Electoral Votes Are Distributed Among States

The allocation of electoral votes is a fundamental aspect of the Electoral College system. Each state's number of electoral votes is determined by its representation in Congress: the sum of its Senators (always two) and Representatives (which varies based on population). This formula ensures every state has at least three electoral votes, while populous states like California and Texas have significantly more.

- **Apportionment Process:** Every ten years, following the national census, the number of Representatives in the House is reapportioned among the states based on population changes. This, in turn, can affect a state's electoral votes.

- **Impact on Smaller States:** The Electoral College often overrepresents smaller states relative to their population because every state, regardless of size, gets at least three electoral votes. This fact underscores the Electoral College's significant impact on the political power of smaller states, making you more aware of the system's implications.

- **District of Columbia:** Under the 23rd Amendment, Washington, D.C., is treated like a state for the Electoral College and is allocated three electoral votes (National Archives).

Winner-Takes-All vs. Proportional Allocation: Explanation of Different Methods States Use

Most states use a "winner-takes-all" system, where the candidate who wins the popular vote in that state receives all of its electoral votes. However, Maine and Nebraska employ a proportional system that allows electoral votes to be split between candidates.

- **Winner-Takes-All System:** This method can lead to a candidate winning the presidency by securing electoral votes in key states, even if they lose the national popular vote. It emphasizes the importance of winning battleground states.

- **Proportional Allocation:** Maine and Nebraska's method awards one electoral vote per congressional district to the candidate who wins that district, with the remaining two votes going to the statewide winner. This can result in a more proportional reflection of the voters' preferences in those states (<u>USAGov Services</u>).

Controversies and Criticisms: Debate over the Fairness of the Electoral College

The Electoral College has been the subject of intense debate and criticism, particularly in recent years when its outcomes have diverged from the national popular vote.

- **Discrepancy Between Popular and Electoral Votes:** Critics argue that the Electoral College can produce undemocratic results, where the candidate who loses the popular vote wins the presidency. This has happened five times in U.S. history, most recently in 2000 and 2016.

- **Swing State Focus:** The system encourages candidates to focus their campaigns on a small number of swing states, potentially neglecting voters in states that are solidly Democratic or Republican.

- **Calls for Reform**: Various reforms have been proposed, including the National Popular Vote Interstate Compact, which aims to ensure the presidency goes to the candidate who wins the popular vote without abolishing the Electoral College altogether (<u>Brennan Center for Justice</u>).

Chapter 3

Voter Registration

Introduction: The Foundation of Civic Participation

Voter registration is the bedrock of electoral participation in the United States, serving as the crucial first step that enables citizens to exercise their right to vote. While voting is often seen as the most direct expression of democracy, the voter registration process determines who participates in that democratic exercise. Registering to vote is not only a legal requirement but also a reflection of a person's active engagement in the civic life of their community. Yet, despite its fundamental importance, voter registration is also one of the most complex and contested aspects of the U.S. electoral system.

The importance of voter registration cannot be overstated. It helps to ensure that elections are conducted fairly by confirming that each voter is eligible and that they vote in the correct precinct. However, the process and requirements for voter registration vary widely across states, leading to significant differences in how accessible or restrictive the process can be. These differences have profound implications for voter turnout, particularly among historically marginalized groups. In this chapter, we will explore the intricacies of voter registration, including eligibility requirements, registration methods, voter roll maintenance, efforts to increase registration, and the challenges and controversies surrounding this critical process.

Eligibility Requirements:

Who Can Register?

To register to vote in the United States, individuals must meet specific eligibility requirements established by state law. These requirements are generally consistent across the country, with some variations.

US Citizenship

The most fundamental requirement for voter registration is U.S. citizenship. Only citizens of the United States are allowed to vote in federal elections, and most states extend this requirement to state and local elections as well. Proof of citizenship, such as birth certificates, passports, or naturalization papers, may be required when registering to vote, particularly in states with strict voter ID laws.

Residency

Voters must be residents of the state in which they wish to register. This requirement ensures that individuals vote in the elections that affect their communities. Residency requirements can vary slightly from state to state. For example, some states require individuals to have lived in the state for a certain period before they are eligible to register, often ranging from 10 to 30 days. Residency can also determine which local races a voter can participate in, such as city council or school board elections.

Age

To register to vote, an individual must be at least 18 by Election Day. However, many states allow citizens to pre-register at 16 or 17 years old, so they are automatically registered when they turn 18. This practice is critical in engaging younger voters early and integrating them into the democratic process.

Non-Felon Status

The rules regarding the voting rights of individuals with felony convictions vary significantly by state. In some states, individuals with felony convictions are permanently disenfranchised unless they receive a pardon or have their rights restored through a specific legal process. In other states, voting rights, including parole and probation, are automatically restored once an individual has completed their sentence. A growing number of states are also considering or have enacted laws to restore voting rights immediately upon release from prison, reflecting a trend toward greater enfranchisement of formerly incarcerated individuals.

Special Cases: Military and Overseas Voters

Special provisions exist for U.S. citizens serving in the military or living abroad. The Uniformed and Overseas Citizens Absentee Voting Act (UOCAVA) ensures that these citizens can register to vote and cast their ballots, even if they are stationed overseas or in a different state. Military and overseas voters often vote by absentee ballot, and special considerations are made to ensure their votes are counted, even if they are submitted from remote or international locations.

Registration Processes:

How to Register

Once eligibility is established, individuals must navigate the voter registration process, which can vary widely depending on the state. Understanding these processes is crucial for ensuring that all eligible citizens can successfully register to vote.

Online Registration

Online voter registration has become popular and convenient in many states, especially for younger voters and those with access to digital technology. Online registration systems typically require voters to enter their personal information and provide a driver's license or state ID number for identity verification. This method is not only convenient but also helps to reduce errors that can occur with paper forms. States that offer online registration have seen significant increases in voter registration rates, particularly among young and mobile populations.

In-Person Registration

Traditional in-person registration remains an important option, especially for those who may not have Internet access or prefer a more personal approach. In-person registration is typically available at government offices, such as the Department of Motor Vehicles (DMV), public assistance, and election offices. In some states, community organizations and advocacy groups also set up registration drives in public spaces to reach a broader audience. In-person registration often provides immediate confirmation of registration, giving voters confidence that their information has been received and processed.

Mail-In Registration

Mail-in registration is another widely used method, particularly for voters who cannot register in person or online. This method involves filling out a registration form, which can be downloaded from the state's election website or obtained from government offices, and mailing it to the local election office. While convenient, mail-in registration can be slower than other methods, and there is a risk of forms being lost or delayed in the mail. Voters need to send in their forms well before the registration deadline to ensure they are processed in time for the election.

Same-Day Registration

Same-day registration, also known as Election Day registration, allows voters to register and cast their ballot on the same day, either during early voting or on Election Day itself. This option is available in a growing number of states and has been shown to increase voter turnout, particularly among young voters, minorities, and individuals who may not have been able to register beforehand. Same-day registration eliminates the barrier of advance registration deadlines, making the voting process more inclusive.

Voter Registration Deadlines

Voter registration deadlines are a critical aspect of the registration process. These deadlines vary by state, with most requiring voters to register several weeks before an election. Some states, particularly those with same-day registration, allow voters to register until Election Day. Missing the registration deadline can disenfranchise potential voters, so individuals must be aware of and adhere to these deadlines.

Voter Roll Maintenance:

Keeping the Lists Accurate

Maintaining accurate voter rolls, or voter registration lists, is essential for the integrity of elections. These lists are the official records of eligible voters in a jurisdiction. They must be regularly updated to reflect changes such as moves, deaths, and changes in legal status. However, the process of maintaining voter rolls is not without controversy.

Updating Voter Rolls

States are responsible for regularly updating their voter rolls to reflect the eligible voting population accurately. This process includes:

- **Address Changes:** When voters move, they must update their registration to reflect their new address. States often receive updates through the DMV, the U.S. Postal Service, or other government agencies. Failure to update an address can result in a voter being assigned to the wrong precinct or, in some cases, being removed from the voter rolls.

- **Deceased Voters:** States remove deceased individuals from voter rolls using information from vital records departments or other official sources. This process helps to prevent voter fraud and ensure that only eligible voters remain on the rolls.

- **Name Changes:** Voters who change their names, often due to marriage or divorce, must update their registration to reflect the new name. This update ensures that the voter's registration matches their identification documents.

Voter Roll Purges

Voter roll purges remove individuals from voter rolls who are believed to be ineligible to vote, often due to inactivity, relocation, or failure to respond to verification notices. While purges are intended to maintain accurate and up-to-date voter rolls, they can sometimes result in the removal of eligible voters. This can happen if the purge process is not carefully managed or voters do not receive or respond to notices in time.

The practice of purging voter rolls has been the subject of significant controversy, particularly when it is perceived as targeting specific groups, such as minorities or low-income voters. In some cases, voters have shown up at the polls only to find that they have been removed from the voter rolls, leading to confusion and potential disenfranchisement.

Addressing Inaccuracies

Inaccuracies in voter rolls can undermine public confidence in the electoral process. Common inaccuracies include outdated addresses, duplicate registrations, or errors in voter information. To address these issues, many states conduct periodic audits of their voter rolls and provide opportunities for voters to update their information. Additionally, voters are encouraged to verify their registration status before elections to ensure their information is accurate and current.

Efforts to Increase Voter Registration

Recognizing the importance of voter registration in ensuring broad electoral participation, various efforts have been made at both the state and federal levels to increase voter registration rates. These efforts include policy reforms, technological innovations, and outreach initiatives.

Automatic Voter Registration (AVR)

Automatic Voter Registration (AVR) is a system where eligible citizens are automatically registered to vote when interacting with certain government agencies, such as the DMV. Unless they opt out, their information is forwarded to election officials, who add them to the voter rolls.

Chapter 4

⬥

The Primary System

Types of Primaries: Open, Closed, Semi-Closed, and Blanket Primaries

Primaries are a crucial part of the U.S. electoral process, serving as how political parties select their candidates for the general election. Several primary systems across the United States have rules and implications for voters and candidates. Understanding the differences between these systems is crucial in choosing candidates.

Closed Primaries

In a closed primary, only registered members of a political party are allowed to vote in that party's primary election. This means that if you are registered as a Democrat, you can only vote in the Democratic primary, and the same goes for Republicans. Closed primaries are designed to ensure that only party members have a say in selecting the party's nominee, which helps to maintain party loyalty and prevents members of other parties from influencing the outcome.

- **Party Loyalty:** Closed primaries encourage party members to stay loyal to their candidates and policies.

- **Voter Registration:** Depending on state laws, voters must declare their party affiliation when they register to vote or before the primary.

- **Impact on Independents:** Independent voters, or those not affiliated with any party, are generally excluded from voting in closed primaries, which can lead to criticism about the inclusivity of this system.

Open Primaries

Open primaries, in contrast, allow all registered voters to participate in a party's primary election, regardless of their party affiliation. On Election Day, voters choose which party they want to vote in, but they can only vote in one primary. This system is more inclusive, allowing independent voters or those who prefer to remain unaffiliated with a particular party to have a voice in selecting candidates.

- **Flexibility for Voters:** Open primaries provide greater flexibility and can lead to higher voter turnout, allowing more people to participate in the primary process.

- **Strategic Voting:** Some voters might choose to vote in the opposite party's primary to influence the selection of a weaker candidate, a tactic known as "crossover voting."

- **Potential for Dilution:** Critics argue that open primaries can dilute the influence of committed party members by allowing non-members to sway the outcome.

Semi-Closed Primaries

Semi-closed primaries are a hybrid system that combines elements of both closed and open primaries. In this system, registered party members can only vote in their own party's primary, but independent voters can choose which primary they want. This approach seeks to balance party loyalty with inclusivity.

- **Inclusivity for Independents:** Semi-closed primaries allow independents to participate, aiming to increase voter engagement without completely opening the primary to all voters.

- **Party Control:** This system still gives party members significant control over the selection process while offering flexibility for unaffiliated voters.

- **Variation by State:** The rules for semi-closed primaries can vary widely by state, with some states requiring independents to declare a party affiliation before voting.

Blanket Primaries

Blanket primaries, or "jungle primaries," allow all voters to vote for any candidate in the primary election regardless of party affiliation. All candidates from all parties are listed on the same ballot, and the top two vote-getters, regardless of party, advance to the general election. This system is designed to encourage candidates to appeal to a broader electorate.

- **Non-Partisan Approach:** Blanket primaries can reduce partisanship by encouraging candidates to appeal to a broader range of voters rather than just their party base.

- **Impact on General Elections:** In some cases, two candidates from the same party may compete against each other in the general election if they receive the most votes in the primary.

- **Criticism and Praise:** While some praise this system for promoting more moderate candidates, others criticize it for potentially shutting out minority party candidates from the general election.

Caucuses vs. Primaries:

How They Differ and Which States Use Each Method

In the United States, both caucuses and primaries are used to select delegates representing a political party at its national convention, where the party's presidential nominee is officially chosen. While both processes serve the same purpose, they differ significantly in how they are conducted and how voters participate. Understanding these differences is crucial to understanding the broader electoral system.

What is a Caucus?

A caucus is a local gathering of party members to discuss and vote on the candidates. Caucuses are often more participatory and involve multiple rounds of voting or deliberation before a final decision is made. This method has a long history in American politics but is now used by fewer states than primaries.

- **Local Meetings**: In a caucus, registered party members meet in local precincts, such as schools or community centers, to discuss the candidates. The process can be lengthy, often lasting several hours.

- **Group Dynamics**: Voters physically gather in groups based on their preferred candidate. If a candidate does not receive a certain percentage of support (usually 15%), their supporters may be asked to join another group or abstain from voting. This process encourages debate and coalition-building.

- **State Examples**: Iowa is the most famous state that uses the caucus system, mainly because it holds the first caucus in the nation during each presidential election cycle. Other states that use caucuses include Nevada and Wyoming, though the number of states using caucuses has declined in recent years.

What is a Primary?

A primary, by contrast, is a more straightforward voting process where party members cast ballots for their preferred candidate, similar to a general election. As discussed in the previous section, primaries can be open, closed, or semi-closed and are typically less time-consuming than caucuses.

- **Secret Ballot Voting**: Primaries use a secret ballot, unlike caucuses, where voters publicly declare their support. This allows voters to choose privately, like voting in a general election.

- **Higher Participation**: Primaries generally have higher voter turnout than caucuses because they are more accessible. Voters can often vote throughout the day without attending a specific meeting or engaging in lengthy discussions.

- **State Examples**: Most states use primary elections to choose their delegates. For instance, New Hampshire holds the first primary in the nation, making it a critical early test for candidates. Other key primary states include California, Texas, and South Carolina.

Differences Between Caucuses and Primaries

While both caucuses and primaries serve to select delegates for the national convention, their processes are distinct, leading to different voter experiences and outcomes. Caucuses involve active participation and deliberation, while primaries offer a more straightforward, private voting process.

- **Participation:** Caucuses require higher engagement, as voters must attend a specific meeting and often engage in public debate. On the other hand, primaries allow for quick, private voting, leading to higher turnout.

- **Time Commitment:** Caucuses can take several hours, as they involve discussion, realignment, and multiple rounds of voting. Primaries are much quicker, as voters cast a ballot and leave.

- **Influence on Outcomes:** Because of their participatory nature, caucuses can sometimes favor candidates with grassroots solid support or organizational strength, as committed supporters are likelier to attend and advocate for their candidate.

States That Use Caucuses and Primaries

While most states now use primary elections, a few continue to hold caucuses, particularly in states with smaller populations or where party rules favor the caucus method. The choice between caucuses and primaries can significantly impact a candidate's strategy, as each method requires different approaches to voter engagement.

- **Caucus States:** As of recent elections, Iowa, Nevada, and Wyoming are among the states that continue to use caucuses, although some states have switched from caucuses to primaries to increase voter participation.

- **Primary States:** Most other states use primaries, including central states like California, New York, and Florida. These states have large numbers of delegates and are crucial in determining the eventual nominee.

Superdelegates and Their Role:

Superdelegates are a unique feature of the Democratic Party's primary process, potentially pivotal in selecting the party's presidential nominee. Unlike regular delegates bound by their state's primary or caucus results, superdelegates can support any candidate, regardless of the outcomes. Understanding the role and influence of superdelegates is essential to grasping the dynamics of the Democratic primary process.

Who Are Superdelegates?

Superdelegates are typically party leaders, elected officials, and other prominent members of the Democratic Party. They include members of the Democratic National Committee (DNC), current and former Presidents, Vice Presidents, members of Congress, and Governors, as well as distinguished party leaders. Their position as superdelegates reflects their standing within the party and their influence in the political landscape.

- **Automatic Delegates:** Unlike regular delegates, superdelegates are not elected through primaries or caucuses. They automatically receive their status based on their position or past contributions to the party.

- **Unbound Voting:** Superdelegates are not bound by the results of the primaries or caucuses in their states. They are free to support whichever candidate they believe is best suited to represent the party in the general election.

- **Number of Superdelegates:** The number of superdelegates can vary from election to election, but they generally comprise around 15% of the total delegate count at the Democratic National Convention.

The Historical Context of Superdelegates

The superdelegate system was introduced in the early 1980s as a response to concerns that the primary process had become too dominated by grassroots activists, potentially leading to the selection of candidates who might struggle in the general election. The party leadership wanted a mechanism to ensure that experienced party officials and elected leaders could have a significant voice in the nomination process.

- **Creation in 1984:** The superdelegate system was first implemented in the 1984 Democratic primary. It was seen as a way to balance rank-and-file voters' influence with party elites, ensuring that the party's nominee would be broadly acceptable to both groups.

- **Controversial Role:** The role of superdelegates has been controversial, particularly in close races where their support could determine the outcome. Critics argue that superdelegates can undermine the democratic process by overriding the will of the voters. At the same time, supporters claim they provide a necessary check to prevent the nomination of unelectable candidates.

Superdelegates in Recent Elections

Superdelegates have played significant roles in several recent Democratic primary contests, most notably in the 2008 and 2016 elections. Their influence can be decisive, especially in tight races where no candidate secures a majority of pledged delegates.

- **2008 Democratic Primary:** During the 2008 primary, the contest between Barack Obama and Hillary Clinton was so close that superdelegates became crucial in determining the nominee. Ultimately, many superdelegates sided with Obama, helping him secure the nomination.

- **2016 Democratic Primary:** 2016 Hillary Clinton entered the Democratic National Convention with a strong lead among pledged delegates and superdelegates, effectively securing her nomination over Bernie Sanders before the convention began. This led to significant criticism from Sanders supporters, who argued that the superdelegate system was undemocratic.

- **Reforms in 2020:** In response to the controversies of previous elections, the Democratic Party reformed the superdelegate system ahead of the 2020 primary. Under the new rules, superdelegates would not vote on the first ballot at the convention unless a candidate had already secured a majority of pledged delegates. This change was designed to reduce the influence of superdelegates and ensure that the nominee would reflect the will of the voters.

The Impact of Superdelegates on the Primary Process

The presence of superdelegates in the Democratic primary process adds a layer of complexity and can influence candidates' strategies. While their power has been curtailed in recent years, they still represent an essential bloc within the party, capable of swinging the nomination in a contested convention.

- **Strategic Considerations:** Candidates often seek to court superdelegates early in the primary process, understanding that their support could be crucial in a close race. This can lead to behind-the-scenes negotiations and endorsements that may not always align with the outcomes of the primaries and caucuses.

- **Debate Over Fairness:** The ongoing debate about the fairness of the superdelegate system reflects broader tensions within the Democratic Party between grassroots activists and the party establishment. Reforms have sought to address these concerns, but the debate over the role of superdelegates is likely to continue in future elections.

Chapter 5

⬥◇⬥

The General Election

Campaigning: How Candidates Compete for Votes

The general election campaign is the climax of the U.S. electoral process, where candidates intensify their efforts to win voters' support nationwide. Campaigning during the general election involves a multifaceted approach, including targeted advertising, strategic messaging, public appearances, debates, and media coverage. This phase is critical as candidates work to solidify their base, sway undecided voters, and ultimately secure enough electoral votes to win the presidency. This section provides an overview of how candidates campaign during the general election, highlighting the strategies, tactics, and critical activities involved in the final push to win over voters. It explains the importance of debates, media coverage, public appearances, and fundraising in shaping the election outcome. Would you like to move on to the next section, or is there anything specific you'd like to adjust?

Strategic Campaign Planning

The foundation of any successful campaign is a well-crafted strategy. Campaigns are meticulously planned, often years in advance, with strategies tailored to maximize a candidate's appeal to key demographics and swing states. This planning involves extensive polling, data analysis, and consultation with political advisors to determine the best approach for reaching and persuading voters.

- **Swing States:** Candidates focus heavily on swing states—states where the outcome is uncertain and could go either way. Winning these states is often crucial to securing the necessary 270 electoral votes.

- **Demographic Targeting:** Campaigns use detailed voter data to target specific demographics, such as suburban women, young voters, or minority groups, tailoring messages that resonate with their concerns and priorities.

- **Ground Game vs. Air War:** The "ground game" refers to grassroots efforts, such as door-to-door canvassing and voter registration drives, while the "air war" involves media advertising, particularly on television and social media.

The Role of Debates

Presidential debates are among the most high-profile events during a general election campaign. They provide candidates a national platform to outline their policies, challenge their opponents, and connect with voters. Debates can significantly influence public perception and often serve as pivotal moments in the campaign.

- **Debate Preparation:** Candidates spend weeks preparing for debates, often engaging in mock debates to refine their arguments and anticipate their opponent's strategies.

- **Influence on Voters:** Debates can be critical in swaying undecided voters, as they provide a direct comparison of the candidates' policies, demeanor, and ability to handle pressure.

- **Notable Debate Moments:** History is filled with memorable debate moments that have swayed elections, such as John F. Kennedy's confident performance against Richard Nixon in 1960, highlighting the growing importance of television in politics.

Media Coverage and Advertising

Media coverage plays a crucial role in shaping a campaign's narrative. Candidates use paid advertising and earned media—news coverage they do not pay for—to reach voters. How the media portrays candidates can significantly impact voter perceptions and the overall direction of the campaign.

- **Paid Advertising:** Campaigns spend millions on television, online, and print media to communicate their message. These ads can be positive, focusing on the candidate's strengths, or negative, attacking their opponent.

- **Social Media:** Recently, social media platforms like Facebook, Twitter, and Instagram have become essential campaign tools. They allow candidates to engage directly with voters and tailor their messages in real-time.

- **News Coverage:** How the media covers a candidate—whether focusing on policy proposals, gaffes, or scandals—can significantly influence public opinion. Candidates often try to shape the news cycle by making strategic announcements or holding press conferences.

Public Appearances and Rallies

Public appearances and rallies are vital for energizing a candidate's base and demonstrating their support among voters. These events allow candidates to connect with voters on a personal level, convey enthusiasm, and solidify their campaign's message.

- **Rallies:** Large rallies are a staple of general election campaigns, especially for populist candidates who thrive on direct interaction with supporters. Rallies are designed to create a sense of momentum and inevitability around a candidate's campaign.

- **Town Halls:** Smaller, more intimate events like town halls allow candidates to engage directly with voters' questions and concerns. These events can help candidates appear more relatable and in touch with everyday Americans.

- **Endorsements and Appearances:** Public endorsements from famous and/or popular figures or fellow politicians can boost a candidate's credibility and expand their appeal. Joint appearances with key endorsers are often used to maximize media coverage and voter attention.

Fundraising and Financial Resources

Fundraising is the lifeblood of any campaign. Candidates must raise significant money to fund their operations, pay for advertising, and maintain a strong ground game. The ability to raise money is often seen as a measure of a candidate's viability and support.

- **Donor Networks:** Successful campaigns cultivate extensive donor networks, ranging from small individual donors to large contributors, including Political Action Committees (PACs) and Super PACs.

- **Fundraising Events:** High-profile fundraising events, often hosted by celebrities or wealthy supporters, can bring significant sums of money and generate positive media coverage.

- **Campaign Finance Laws:** Campaign finance laws regulate how much money individuals and organizations can donate to a campaign and how that money can be spent. Despite these regulations, there are often debates about money's influence in politics and the need for reform.

Voting Day:

What Happens on Election Day

Election Day is the culmination of months, sometimes years, of campaigning. It is the day voters across the United States head to the polls to cast their ballots and determine the outcome of various races, including the presidency, congressional seats, and local offices. Understanding what happens on this day, from the opening of polling places to the closing of the polls and the counting of the votes, is crucial for appreciating the mechanics of the electoral process.

Polling Locations and Procedures

Polling locations are the physical sites where voters cast their ballots on Election Day. These locations are carefully selected and managed to ensure all eligible voters can participate in the election. The procedures followed at polling locations are designed to maintain the integrity and security of the voting process.

- **Polling Place Locations:** Polling places are typically set up in public buildings such as schools, community centers, and churches. Each precinct—a specific geographic area within a voting district—has a designated polling place where its residents vote.

- **Check-In Process:** Upon arriving at the polling place, voters must check in with election officials. This process typically involves verifying the voter's identity and checking them against the voter registration list. In some states, voters must present an ID; in others, simply stating their name and address may suffice.

- **Ballot Types:** Depending on the state and the specific election, voters may use different ballots, including paper ballots, optical scan ballots, or electronic voting machines. Voters mark their choices on the ballot, which is then cast into a secure box or electronically recorded.

Voter Assistance and Accessibility

A fundamental principle of the electoral process is ensuring that all eligible voters can access polling places and cast their votes. Various measures are in place to assist voters, including those with disabilities, language barriers, or other needs.

- **Assistance at Polling Places:** Voters who need help can request assistance from poll workers or bring someone to help mark their ballot. In many states, polling places must have equipment or services available to assist voters with disabilities, such as accessible voting machines or ballots in braille.

- **Provisional Ballots:** If a voter's eligibility is questioned, such as if their name does not appear on the voter list, they may be offered a provisional ballot. These ballots are set aside and counted only after election officials have confirmed the voter's eligibility.

- **Language Assistance:** In areas with significant populations of non-English speakers, federal law requires that ballots and voting materials be provided in languages other than English. Additionally, bilingual poll workers may be available to assist voters who need help understanding the process.

Ensuring Fairness and Security

Maintaining the fairness and security of the election is a top priority on Election Day. Various procedures and measures are in place to ensure that all votes are cast and counted accurately and that the process is free from fraud or intimidation.

- **Election Monitors:** Nonpartisan observers and representatives from political parties may be present at polling locations to monitor the voting process. These monitors ensure that the election is conducted fairly and report any irregularities.

- **Security Measures:** Polling places are often staffed with law enforcement or security personnel to prevent disruptions. Additionally, voting equipment is tested and certified before Election Day to ensure it functions correctly.

- **Voter Intimidation Laws:** Voter intimidation is prohibited, and election officials are trained to recognize and address any harassment or coercion at the polls. Voters who feel threatened or unsafe can report issues to local election authorities or law enforcement.

The Closing of Polls and the Start of Vote Counting

When the polls close, counting the votes begins. The procedures for closing the polls and counting the votes are designed to ensure accuracy, transparency, and prompt reporting of results.

- **Closing Procedures:** At the end of voting hours, poll workers close the polling place, ensuring that all voters in line by the closing time are allowed to cast their ballots. The voting machines are then shut down, and the ballots are secured for transport to counting centers.

- **Immediate Count:** In many locations, the counting of votes begins immediately after the polls close. Depending on the jurisdiction's procedures, election officials tally the ballots on-site or at a central location. The results from each precinct are then reported to the county or state election office.

- **Reporting Results:** Preliminary results are often reported within hours of the polls closing, giving the public and candidates an early indication of the election's outcome. However, final official results may take days or weeks to certify, especially in close races or when many absentee or provisional ballots are involved.

Dear Reader,

Thank you for reading "Two Paths Diverged – The Highs, Lows, and Hows Of Hiking."

As an independent author, your support means everything to me. If you enjoyed reading these pages, please consider leaving a review on the platform where you purchased it. Your feedback is invaluable and helps other readers discover this book.

Your honest review encourages me and helps me grow as a writer. Whether you loved it, found it thought-provoking, or have constructive criticism to share, I genuinely appreciate your input.

To leave a review, scan the QR code below to be taken to the Amazon page. Just a minute of your time and consideration are greatly appreciated.

Again, thank you for being a part of this literary adventure. I am honored.

Sincerely,
Brian Eby

Chapter 6

The Electoral College

Electoral Votes Allocation:

How Electoral Votes Are Distributed Among States

The Electoral College is a unique and critical component of the U.S. electoral system, determining the outcome of presidential elections. One of the key elements of this system is the allocation of electoral votes among the states. Understanding how these votes are distributed provides insight into the mechanics of U.S. presidential elections and the relative influence of different states in the election process.

The Basics of Electoral Vote Allocation

Each state's total representation in Congress determines its electoral votes: the sum of its Senators and Representatives. Every state is allocated two electoral votes for its Senators, as each has two Senators regardless of population. Additionally, each state receives electoral votes equivalent to the number of its Representatives based on the state's population determined by the most recent U.S. Census.

- **Total Number of Electoral Votes:** The Electoral College has 538 total electoral votes. This number includes 100 votes for the Senate (two per state), 435 votes for the House of Representatives (apportioned based on population), and three for Washington, D.C., which was granted electoral votes by the 23rd Amendment.

- **Minimum Allocation:** Every state is guaranteed at least three electoral votes (two for its Senators and one for its Representatives), even the least populous states like Wyoming, Vermont, and Alaska.

- **Population Impact:** Larger states like California, Texas, and Florida have more electoral votes because they have larger populations, resulting in more Representatives. For example, as of the most recent apportionment, California has 54 electoral votes, Texas has 40, and Florida has 30.

The Apportionment Process

The apportionment of Representatives—and, by extension, electoral votes—occurs every ten years following the national Census. The Census counts the population of each state, which is then used to determine how many seats each state will have in the House of Representatives. This process can lead to shifts in electoral vote allocation as states gain or lose Representatives based on population changes.

- **Census Data:** The U.S. Census Bureau conducts a national census every ten years, which serves as the basis for reapportioning the 435 seats in the House of Representatives. States that experience significant population growth may gain additional seats, while states with stagnant or declining populations may lose seats.

- **Reapportionment Effects:** After each Census, some states may gain electoral votes, increasing their influence in presidential elections, while others may lose votes. For example, following the 2020 Census, Texas gained two electoral votes due to its population growth, while states like New York and California each lost one electoral vote due to slower population growth relative to other states.

The Role of the District of Columbia

The 23rd Amendment to the Constitution allocates three electoral votes to the District of Columbia, though it is not a state. This ensures that residents of the nation's capital have representation in presidential elections, though D.C. does not have voting representation in Congress.

- **23rd Amendment:** Ratified in 1961, the 23rd Amendment granted Washington, D.C., the right to participate in presidential elections by allocating it three electoral votes, the minimum number that any state can have.

- **Impact on Elections:** Although D.C. has a relatively small population and thus only three electoral votes, it consistently participates in the electoral process, typically voting heavily Democratic in recent elections.

The Influence of Electoral Vote Allocation on Presidential Campaigns

- The distribution of electoral votes heavily influences presidential candidates' campaigns. Candidates tend to focus on states with significant electoral votes and battleground states with uncertain outcomes. This strategy reflects the "winner-takes-all" nature of most states' electoral vote allocation, where winning the popular vote in a state means securing all of its electoral votes.

- **Swing States:** States with a large number of electoral votes and competitive political landscapes, known as swing states, receive significant attention from candidates. These states, such as Florida, Pennsylvania, and Ohio, often determine the election outcome.

- **Campaign Strategies:** Candidates may spend less time in states where the outcome is considered a foregone conclusion, such as heavily Democratic or Republican states, and instead focus their resources on persuading voters in more competitive regions.

Winner-Takes-All vs. Proportional Allocation:

Different Methods States Use

How states allocate their electoral votes is critical in determining the outcome of U.S. presidential elections. Most states use a "winner-takes-all" system, while a few employ a proportional allocation method. Understanding these systems is essential to comprehend how the Electoral College operates and its impact on election strategies.

Winner-Takes-All System

The "winner-takes-all" system is the predominant method 48 states and the District of Columbia use to allocate their electoral votes. In this system, the candidate who receives the most popular votes in a state wins all of that state's electoral votes. This approach amplifies the importance of swing states and can lead to situations where a candidate wins the Electoral College while losing the national popular vote.

- **Statewide Victory:** In the winner-takes-all system, a candidate only needs to win a plurality of the vote in a state to claim all of its electoral votes. For example, if Candidate A wins 51% of the vote in Florida, they receive all 30 of Florida's electoral votes, while Candidate B receives none, even if they secured 49%.

- **Impact on Campaigns:** This system encourages presidential candidates to focus on a few key battleground states where the outcome is uncertain, and all electoral votes are up for grabs. As a result, states with more predictable outcomes, such as heavily

Democratic California or heavily Republican Alabama, often receive less attention during the campaign.

Proportional Allocation System

Maine and Nebraska use a proportional allocation system, unlike the winner-takes-all approach. This system allows electoral votes to be split between candidates based on their performance in the state's congressional districts and the statewide vote.

- **Maine and Nebraska's Method:** In these states, two electoral votes are awarded to the candidate who wins the statewide popular vote, while one electoral vote is awarded for each congressional district won. This means that multiple candidates can earn electoral votes from the same state.

- **Example of Proportional Results:** In the 2020 election, Nebraska awarded three electoral votes to Donald Trump, who won the statewide vote and two of its three congressional districts. The remaining electoral vote went to Joe Biden, who won Nebraska's 2nd Congressional District, which includes Omaha.

- **Impact on Campaigns:** The proportional system can lead to more nuanced campaigning in Maine and Nebraska, where candidates may focus on specific congressional districts rather than the state. However, because these states have relatively few electoral votes, their overall impact on the election outcome is limited.

Advantages and Disadvantages of Each System

Both the winner-takes-all and proportional allocation systems have advantages and disadvantages, and each influences election outcomes and campaign strategies in different ways.

- **Advantages of Winner-Takes-All:**

  o **Clarity:** This system provides a clear, decisive outcome in each state, contributing to the efficiency of the Electoral College process.

  o **Strong Incentive:** It incentivizes candidates to focus on winning entire states, which can simplify the electoral strategy.

- **Disadvantages of Winner-Takes-All:**

  o **Disenfranchisement:** Voters who support the losing candidate in a state may feel disenfranchised because their votes do not contribute to the overall electoral count.

  o **Disparity Between Popular and Electoral Vote:** This system can result in a candidate winning the presidency without winning the national popular vote, as seen in the 2000 and 2016 elections.

- **Advantages of Proportional Allocation:**

  o **Fairer Representation:** This system allows for a more accurate reflection of voters' preferences within a state, as electoral votes are divided rather than awarded in a block.

   o **Potential for Broader Campaigning:** Candidates may be encouraged to campaign in parts of a state that might otherwise be overlooked in a winner-takes-all system.

- **Disadvantages of Proportional Allocation:**

   o **Complexity:** The proportional method can complicate the voting process and counting electoral votes, potentially leading to a less clear outcome on election night.

   o **Limited Impact:** Because only two states use this method, its overall effect on the election is minimal compared to the widespread use of the winner-takes-all system.

The Debate Over Electoral Vote Allocation

The debate over how electoral votes should be allocated is ongoing, with some advocating a shift to a national popular vote or other reforms that could address the current system's perceived shortcomings.

- **Arguments for Reform:** Critics of the winner-takes-all system argue that it undermines the principle of one person, one vote, and leads to a disproportionate focus on swing states. Reform proposals include the National Popular Vote Interstate Compact, which ensures that the candidate who wins the most votes nationwide becomes president, regardless of the Electoral College outcome.

- **Resistance to Change:** Proponents of the Electoral College and the winner-takes-all system argue that they protect the interests of smaller states and maintain the federalist structure of the U.S. government. They also contend that the current system promotes stability and a clear mandate for the winning candidate.

Controversies and Criticisms:

Debate over the Fairness of the Electoral College

The Electoral College has been a subject of debate since its inception. Critics argue that it is an outdated and undemocratic system, while supporters contend that it protects the interests of smaller states and maintains a balance in the federal system. Understanding these controversies is essential to grasping the complexities and challenges of the U.S. presidential election process.

Discrepancy Between the Popular Vote and the Electoral College

One of the most significant criticisms of the Electoral College is that it can—and has—resulted in a candidate winning the presidency despite losing the national popular vote. This discrepancy has occurred five times in U.S. history, most recently in the 2000 and 2016 elections. Critics argue that this undermines the principle of "one person, one vote" and can lead to questions about the legitimacy of the election outcome.

- **Historical Instances:** In the 2000 election, George W. Bush won the presidency by securing 271 electoral votes despite losing the popular vote to Al Gore by over 500,000 votes. Similarly, in 2016, Donald Trump won the Electoral College with 304 votes while losing the popular vote to Hillary Clinton by nearly 3 million votes.

- **Impact on Voter Perception:** These instances have led to significant public outcry and calls for reform, with many voters feeling that their voices were not adequately represented in the outcome. This has also fueled debates about the democratic legitimacy of the Electoral College.

The Influence of Swing States

Another major criticism of the Electoral College is that it disproportionately focuses on a small number of swing states, or battleground states, where the election outcome is uncertain. As a result, presidential candidates often concentrate their campaign efforts on these states, potentially neglecting voters in states where the outcome is more predictable.

- **Swing State Strategy:** States like Florida, Pennsylvania, and Ohio frequently receive significant attention from candidates because winning these states is often crucial to securing the 270 electoral votes needed for victory. This focus can lead to a situation where voters' concerns in these states are prioritized over those in non-swing states.

- **Neglect of Safe States:** States that are reliably Democratic or Republican, such as California or Alabama, often receive less attention during the campaign because their outcomes are seen as foregone conclusions. This can leave voters in these states feeling overlooked and less engaged in the electoral process.

Disenfranchisement of Minority Voters

The structure of the Electoral College can also disenfranchise minority voters, particularly in states where they make up a significant portion of the population but are consistently outvoted by the majority. In winner-takes-all states, the votes of these minority populations may not be reflected in the electoral outcome, effectively rendering them powerless in the presidential election.

- **Racial Disparities:** Studies have shown that the Electoral College can exacerbate racial disparities in political representation. For example, in states with large minority populations that tend to vote Democratic, if the state votes Republican, those minority votes do not contribute to the overall electoral count.

- **Impact on Policy:** This dynamic can lead to a lack of political attention to issues that disproportionately affect minority communities, as candidates may prioritize voters' concerns in more competitive or demographically homogeneous states.

Calls for Reform and Alternatives

Given these controversies, numerous calls have been made to reform or abolish the Electoral College. Proposals for reform range from adopting the National Popular Vote Interstate Compact to amending the Constitution to replace the Electoral College with a direct popular vote system.

- **National Popular Vote Interstate Compact:** This initiative ensures that the candidate who wins the national popular vote becomes president, regardless of the Electoral College outcome. States that join the compact agree to award their electoral votes to the national candidate who wins the popular vote. However, the compact only takes effect if states totaling 270 electoral votes join.

- **Constitutional Amendment:** Abolishing the Electoral College would require a constitutional amendment. This challenging process requires the approval of two-thirds of both houses of Congress and ratification by three-fourths of the states. Despite widespread support for reform, particularly in the wake of the 2000 and 2016 elections, achieving this level of consensus remains difficult.

- **Proportional Representation:** Another proposed reform is adopting proportional allocation of electoral votes in all states, similar to the systems used by Maine and Nebraska. This approach would more accurately reflect the popular vote within each state but still operate within the framework of the Electoral College.

The Defense of the Electoral College

Despite the criticisms, many argue that the Electoral College is essential to the U.S. political system. Supporters contend that it preserves the federal structure of the government, protects the interests of smaller states, and contributes to the stability of the electoral process by ensuring a clear and decisive outcome.

- **Federalism:** The Electoral College is a key component of the federalist system. It balances the power between states with varying populations and ensures smaller states have a voice in the presidential election.

- **Preventing Regionalism:** Proponents argue that the Electoral College prevents candidates from focusing solely on populated urban areas, forcing them to campaign in diverse regions nationwide. This is believed to encourage a broader, more inclusive approach to governance.

- **Stability:** By requiring a majority of electoral votes to win, the system reduces the likelihood of contested or inconclusive elections, contributing to the overall stability of the U.S. political system.

Chapter 7

Voting Technology and Security

Voting Machines: Different Types of Machines and Their Use Across States

The technology used in voting has evolved significantly over the years, transitioning from paper ballots to a range of electronic systems designed to increase efficiency, accuracy, and accessibility. However, with these advancements come security, reliability, and voter confidence challenges. Understanding the different types of voting machines used across the United States is essential for appreciating the complexities of modern elections.

Types of Voting Machines

Several voting machines are used in U.S. elections, each with its method of capturing and counting votes. The most common types are optical scan machines, direct recording electronic (DRE) machines, and ballot marking devices (BMDs).

- **Optical Scan Machines**: These machines read paper ballots marked by voters, either by filling in bubbles or connecting arrows. The ballots are then fed into an optical scanner, which records the votes. Optical scan machines are widely used because they provide a paper trail that can be audited in case of discrepancies.

- **Direct Recording Electronic (DRE) Machines**: DRE machines allow voters to vote directly on an electronic interface like a touchscreen or a keypad. The machine records the vote electronically; sometimes, a paper record is printed for verification. DREs were popular for a time but have faced criticism due to concerns about security vulnerabilities and the lack of a reliable paper trail in some models.

- **Ballot Marking Devices (BMDs)**: BMDs are a hybrid system that combines electronic voting with a paper ballot. Voters use a touchscreen or other electronic interface to make their selections, and the machine then prints out a paper ballot that reflects those choices. The voter can review the ballot before it is scanned and counted by an optical scanner. BMDs are seen as a way to combine the accessibility of electronic voting with the security of a paper trail.

Adoption of Voting Machines Across States

The type of voting machine used varies widely across states and even within states, depending on the jurisdiction. Factors such as the size of the voting population, budget constraints, and security concerns influence the choice of voting technology.

- **State-Level Decisions:** In some states, the decision on which type of voting machine to use is made at the state level, leading to uniformity across all counties. Local jurisdictions can choose their systems in others, resulting in a patchwork of different technologies within a single state.

- **Examples of Use:** Since recent elections, many states have moved away from DRE machines without a paper trail due to concerns about security and reliability. States like Georgia and South Carolina have implemented statewide systems using BMDs. In contrast, others, like Oregon and Washington, rely heavily on vote-by-mail systems, which use optical scan machines to count paper ballots.

- **Urban vs. Rural:** Urban areas, with larger populations and higher voter turnout, may require more sophisticated or numerous voting machines to handle the volume, while rural areas might use simpler systems. This disparity can lead to differences in voting experiences and the speed of vote counting.

Security Concerns and Challenges

With the rise of electronic voting systems, voting machine security and integrity concerns have become more prominent. Issues such as hacking, machine malfunctions, and the potential for tampering have led to increased scrutiny and calls for enhanced security measures.

- **Vulnerability to Hacking**: Security experts have demonstrated that some electronic voting machines, particularly older models, are vulnerable to hacking. This has raised fears about potential interference in elections, whether by domestic actors or foreign adversaries.

- **Malfunctions and Errors**: Voting machines are complex technology; like all machines, they can malfunction. Errors in vote recording or counting can occur, leading to disputes and the need for recounts or audits. High-profile examples of voting machine errors have fueled public skepticism about the reliability of electronic voting.

- **Mitigating Risks**: To address these concerns, many states have implemented post-election audits, such as risk-limiting audits, which compare paper records to electronic results to ensure accuracy. Additionally, using machines that produce a voter-verifiable paper trail has become a standard best practice to enhance security and transparency.

The Future of Voting Technology

As technology evolves, so will the tools used in elections. Emerging technologies, such as blockchain and advanced cryptography, offer the potential to secure and streamline the voting process further. Still, they also come with their own set of challenges and risks.

- **Blockchain Voting**: Blockchain technology, known for its use in cryptocurrencies, has been proposed to create a secure and transparent voting system. The decentralized nature of blockchain could theoretically make it more resistant to tampering, though concerns about scalability and accessibility remain.

- **Mobile Voting**: Some jurisdictions have experimented with mobile voting, allowing voters to cast ballots using their smartphones or other devices. While this could increase accessibility and turnout, particularly among younger voters and those with disabilities, it raises significant security concerns.

- **Continuous Improvement**: The need for ongoing investment in secure, reliable voting technology is precise. As threats evolve, so must the measures taken to protect the integrity of elections, ensuring that all voters can trust the systems used to record and count their votes.

Election Security:

Measures Taken to Secure Elections from Tampering and Fraud

Ensuring the security of elections is a fundamental concern in maintaining public trust in the democratic process. As voting technology has evolved, so have the threats and challenges associated with securing elections from tampering and fraud. This section explores the various measures implemented to protect the integrity of the electoral process, including preventive strategies and reactive safeguards.

Securing Voting Machines and Systems

Election officials prioritize the security of voting machines and systems. Given the complexity and variety of voting technologies used across the United States, multiple layers of security are necessary to protect against potential vulnerabilities.

- **Pre-Election Testing:** Before any election, voting machines undergo rigorous testing to ensure they function correctly. This includes logic and accuracy tests to verify that machines record and count votes accurately. These tests are often conducted publicly to increase transparency and trust.

- **Software and Firmware Security:** Voting machines and their software are subject to strict security protocols. This includes using certified software that has been tested for vulnerabilities and regular updates to protect against known security threats. Firmware, the permanent software programmed into the machine, is also protected against unauthorized modifications.

- **Physical Security:** Voting machines are stored and transported under secure conditions, with measures in place to prevent tampering. This includes using seals, locks, secure storage facilities, and chain-of-custody procedures that track the movement of machines from storage to polling locations.

Protecting Against Cyber Threats

Cyber attack threats have grown as elections have increasingly relied on digital infrastructure. Protecting election systems from hacking, phishing, and other cyber threats is essential to maintaining the integrity of the voting process.

- **Cybersecurity Partnerships:** The U.S. government has partnered with state and local election officials to enhance cybersecurity. The Cybersecurity and Infrastructure Security Agency (CISA) provides resources and support to help secure election infrastructure, including risk assessments, threat intelligence, and incident response planning.

- **Monitoring and Detection:** Election systems are monitored for signs of unauthorized access or tampering. This includes network monitoring, intrusion detection systems, and the use of cybersecurity experts to identify and respond to potential threats in real-time.

- **Resilience Measures:** To protect against the impact of a cyber attack, election officials implement resilience measures such as data backups, redundant systems, and contingency planning. These measures ensure the election can continue without disruption or data loss, even if a system is compromised.

Safeguarding Against Voter Fraud

While instances of voter fraud are infrequent, safeguards are in place to prevent and detect any fraudulent activity that could compromise the fairness of an election. These measures are designed to protect against both in-person and absentee ballot fraud.

- **Voter Identification:** Many states require voters to present identification at the polls to verify their identity. The acceptable ID types vary by state, but the goal is to ensure that each vote cast is legitimate. Critics argue that strict ID laws can disenfranchise certain voter groups, leading to ongoing debates about the balance between security and accessibility.

- **Absentee Ballot Verification:** Absentee ballots are subject to rigorous verification processes, including signature matching, address confirmation, and checks against voter rolls to ensure that each ballot is valid. These measures help prevent double voting and other forms of absentee ballot fraud.

- **Poll Worker Training:** Poll workers receive training on recognizing and addressing potential instances of voter fraud or misconduct at polling places. This includes protocols for handling suspicious activity, such as voters attempting to cast multiple ballots or impersonating others.

Post-Election Audits and Recounts

Post-election audits and recounts serve as essential safeguards to verify the accuracy of election results. These processes help ensure that the reported outcomes reflect the valid will of the voters and provide an opportunity to correct any errors that may have occurred during the counting process.

- **Risk-Limiting Audits:** A risk-limiting audit (RLA) is a post-election audit that uses statistical methods to confirm the accuracy of election outcomes. RLAs involve manually checking a sample of ballots and comparing them to the reported results. If discrepancies are found, the audit may be expanded until the accuracy of the results is confirmed.

- **Automatic Recounts:** In some states, an automatic recount is triggered if the margin of victory falls within a certain threshold, typically 0.5% or less. Recounts involve a thorough review of the ballots, either by machine or hand, to ensure that the results are accurate and that no votes were missed or miscounted.

- **Transparency and Public Confidence:** Both audits and recounts are often conducted transparently, with observers from political parties, the media, and the public allowed to witness the process. This transparency is critical to maintaining public confidence in the electoral system.

Challenges in the Digital Age:

The Urgent issues of Hacking, Disinformation, and Cybersecurity Threats

As voting systems have increasingly moved into the digital realm, new challenges have emerged that threaten the security and integrity of elections. The digital age has introduced vulnerabilities not present in traditional paper-based voting systems, making it crucial for election officials to stay ahead of potential threats. This section explores elections' critical challenges in the digital age, including hacking, disinformation campaigns, and broader cybersecurity threats.

The Threat of Hacking

One of the most significant concerns in the digital age is the threat of hacking, which has the potential to disrupt the election process, alter results, or undermine public confidence in the system, whether it's state-sponsored or independent cyber attackers.

- **Targeted Systems:** Voting machines, voter registration databases, and the systems used to report election results are all potential targets for hackers. If successfully breached, these systems could be manipulated to change vote totals, delete or alter voter records, or spread disinformation about the election's status.

- **High-Profile Incidents:** The 2016 U.S. presidential election highlighted the vulnerabilities of election infrastructure to foreign interference. Reports revealed that Russian operatives attempted to infiltrate voter registration systems in multiple states, raising alarms about the potential for future attacks.

- **Defensive Measures:** In response to these threats, election officials have bolstered cybersecurity defenses, including implementing more robust encryption, multi-factor authentication, and more rigorous security protocols for accessing sensitive systems. Continuous monitoring and quick response teams have also been established to address potential breaches in real-time.

Disinformation Campaigns

Disinformation campaigns are another significant challenge in the digital age. These campaigns aim to spread false or misleading information to influence voter behavior, sow discord, or delegitimize the election process. Social media platforms have become critical battlegrounds for these efforts.

- **Types of Disinformation:** Disinformation can take many forms, including fake news articles, misleading social media posts, and doctored images or videos. These campaigns often target vulnerable populations or exploit existing social divisions.

- **Impact on Voter Behavior:** Disinformation can lead to voter suppression by spreading false information about voting procedures, such as incorrect polling locations or dates. It can also polarize public opinion, increasing partisanship and mistrust in the electoral process.

- **Combatting Disinformation:** Efforts to combat disinformation include fact-checking services, public awareness campaigns, and partnerships between social media companies and government agencies to identify and remove false content. Additionally, voters are encouraged to verify information from reliable sources before sharing or acting on it.

Cybersecurity Threats to Election Infrastructure

Beyond hacking and disinformation, election infrastructure faces a broad range of cybersecurity threats that could disrupt the voting process or compromise the integrity of election results. These threats require comprehensive strategies to protect the entire electoral system.

- **Phishing Attacks**: Phishing attacks, in which attackers trick users into providing sensitive information or clicking on malicious links, are a common threat to election officials and volunteers. They can lead to unauthorized access to election systems or the installation of malware.

- **Distributed Denial of Service (DDoS) Attacks**: DDoS attacks involve overwhelming a system with traffic to the point where it becomes inaccessible. Such attacks could target websites that report election results or provide voter information during an election, leading to confusion and delays.

- **Supply Chain Vulnerabilities**: The software and hardware used in voting systems are often produced by third-party vendors, which can introduce vulnerabilities if those vendors are not adequately secured. Ensuring that all components of election systems are secure, from the manufacturers to the end users, is a critical challenge.

- **Incident Response**: To address these threats, election officials must have robust incident response plans. These plans must include rapid detection of breaches, clear communication strategies, and coordination with federal agencies like the Cybersecurity and Infrastructure Security Agency (CISA) to mitigate the impact of any attacks.

The Role of Public Trust and Transparency

Maintaining public trust in the electoral process is crucial, especially in the face of the challenges of the digital age. Transparency in how elections are conducted and results are verified is vital in ensuring voters' confidence in the outcomes.

- **Transparency Measures:** Transparency can be enhanced by making information about election security measures publicly available, conducting open post-election audits, and ensuring that the processes for counting and verifying votes are visible to observers from all parties.

- **Public Education:** It is essential to educate the public about the realities of election security, potential threats, and the steps to mitigate them. An informed electorate is less likely to fall victim to disinformation and more likely to trust the results of a secure and transparent election.

- **Building Resilience:** Encouraging resilience among voters and election officials alike—through training, preparedness drills, and a culture of vigilance—helps ensure that elections' integrity is maintained even in the face of digital threats.

Chapter 8

The Role of Third Parties

Third-Party Candidates:

Impact of Third-Party Candidates on Elections

Third-party candidates have long played a unique and sometimes disruptive role in American elections. While the U.S. political system is predominantly a two-party system, with Democrats and Republicans dominating most electoral contests, third-party candidates have the potential to influence election outcomes, shape political discourse, and introduce new ideas into the political arena. Understanding the impact of third-party candidates is essential for a comprehensive view of the U.S. electoral process.

History of Third-Party Candidates in U.S. Elections

Third-party candidates have been part of the American political landscape since the republic's early days. Although these candidates rarely win primary elections, their influence can be significant, especially in close races where they can draw votes away from the major party candidates.

- **Early Examples:** One of the earliest and most successful third-party candidates was Theodore Roosevelt, who ran for president in 1912 under the Progressive Party (also known as the Bull Moose Party). Roosevelt, a former Republican president, secured 27% of the popular vote and won 88 electoral votes, effectively splitting the Republican vote and handing the election to Democrat Woodrow Wilson.

- **Modern Third-Party Candidates:** More recent examples include Ross Perot, who ran as an independent candidate in 1992 and 1996, and Ralph Nader, who ran as the Green Party candidate in 2000. Perot's 1992 campaign was particularly impactful, as he won 19% of the popular vote, one of the highest totals ever for a third-party candidate in the modern era.

- **Spoiler Effect:** Third-party candidates are often accused of being "spoilers," potentially tipping the balance in closely contested elections. For example, some analysts argue that Ralph Nader's candidacy in 2000 siphoned off enough votes from Democrat Al Gore to enable Republican George W. Bush to win the presidency.

The Influence of Third-Party Platforms

While third-party candidates rarely win elections, they can exert significant influence by highlighting specific issues that the major parties may ignore. These candidates often advocate for policies or reforms that eventually get adopted by the major parties or become central to the national political debate.

- **Policy Innovation:** Third parties often introduce innovative or controversial policy ideas that challenge the status quo. For instance, the Populist Party in the late 19th century pushed for policies like the direct election of Senators, a graduated income tax, and banking reform, many of which were later adopted by the major parties.

- **Shaping the Debate:** By focusing on niche or emerging issues, third-party candidates can force significant parties to address these topics to appeal to voters. The Green Party, for example, has been instrumental in pushing environmental issues into the mainstream political discourse, even though it has not won major elections.

- **Influencing Major Party Platforms:** Sometimes, the success of third-party candidates in highlighting specific issues leads to these issues being incorporated into the major parties' platforms. This can be seen in how both significant parties eventually took up many ideas championed by third-party movements like the Progressives or the Populists.

The Challenges Faced by Third-Party Candidates

Despite their potential impact, third-party candidates face significant obstacles in the U.S. electoral system, which is designed to favor the two major parties. These challenges include ballot access, media coverage, and the "wasted vote" syndrome.

- **Ballot Access:** Third-party candidates face a significant hurdle in getting on the ballot in all 50 states. Each state has its requirements, often involving collecting thousands of signatures, which can be costly and time-consuming.

- **Media Coverage:** Third-party candidates typically receive less media coverage than their major-party counterparts, making it difficult to reach a broad audience. This lack of exposure can contribute to lower voter awareness and support.

- **Wasted Vote Syndrome:** Many voters are reluctant to support third-party candidates because they believe these candidates have little chance of winning. This phenomenon, known as the "wasted vote" syndrome, discourages people from voting for third-party candidates, even if they align more closely with their views.

The Impact on Electoral Outcomes

In some instances, third-party candidates can have a decisive impact on electoral outcomes, particularly in closely contested races. This influence can manifest in various ways, from drawing votes away from major party candidates to altering the strategies of the major parties.

- **Election Spoilers:** In addition to Ralph Nader in 2000, another notable example of a potential "spoiler" effect was the candidacy of Ross Perot in 1992. While Perot did not win any electoral votes, his strong showing is believed to have split the conservative vote, contributing to Bill Clinton's victory over incumbent President George H.W. Bush.

- **Strategic Shifts:** The presence of a robust third-party candidate can force major parties to adjust their strategies, either by adopting some of the third party's positions or by focusing on different issues to differentiate themselves. This can lead to shifts in the political landscape, even if the third-party candidate does not win.

Third-party candidates have long played a unique and sometimes disruptive role in American elections. While the U.S. political system is predominantly a two-party system, with Democrats and Republicans dominating most electoral contests, third-party candidates have the potential to influence election outcomes, shape political discourse, and introduce new ideas into the political arena. Understanding the impact of third-party candidates is essential for a comprehensive view of the U.S. electoral process.

The History of Third-Party Candidates in U.S. Elections

Third-party candidates have been part of the American political landscape since the republic's early days. Although these candidates rarely win primary elections, their influence can be significant, especially in close races where they can draw votes away from the major party candidates.

- **Early Examples:** One of the earliest and most successful third-party candidates was Theodore Roosevelt, who ran for president in 1912 under the Progressive Party (also known as the Bull Moose Party). Roosevelt, a former Republican president, secured 27% of the popular vote and won 88 electoral votes, effectively splitting the Republican vote and handing the election to Democrat Woodrow Wilson.

- **Modern Third-Party Candidates:** More recent examples include Ross Perot, who ran as an independent candidate in 1992 and 1996, and Ralph Nader, who ran as the Green Party candidate in 2000. Perot's 1992 campaign was particularly impactful, as he won 19% of the popular vote, one of the highest totals ever for a third-party candidate in the modern era.

- **Spoiler Effect:** Third-party candidates are often accused of being "spoilers," potentially tipping the balance in closely contested elections. For example, some analysts argue that Ralph Nader's candidacy in 2000 siphoned off enough votes from Democrat Al Gore to enable Republican George W. Bush to win the presidency.

The Influence of Third-Party Platforms

While third-party candidates rarely win elections, they can exert significant influence by highlighting specific issues that the major parties may ignore. These candidates often advocate for policies or reforms that eventually get adopted by the major parties or become central to the national political debate.

- **Policy Innovation:** Third parties often introduce innovative or controversial policy ideas that challenge the status quo. For instance, the Populist Party in the late 19th century pushed for policies like the direct election of Senators, a graduated income tax, and banking reform, many of which were later adopted by the major parties.

- **Shaping the Debate:** By focusing on niche or emerging issues, third-party candidates can force significant parties to address these topics to appeal to voters. The Green Party, for example, has been instrumental in pushing environmental issues into the mainstream political discourse, even though it has not won major elections.

- **Influencing Major Party Platforms:** Sometimes, the success of third-party candidates in highlighting specific issues leads to these issues being incorporated into the major parties' platforms. This can be seen in how both significant parties eventually took up many ideas championed by third-party movements like the Progressives or the Populists.

The Challenges Faced by Third-Party Candidates

Despite their potential impact, third-party candidates face significant obstacles in the U.S. electoral system, which is designed to favor the two major parties. These challenges include ballot access, media coverage, and the "wasted vote" syndrome.

- **Ballot Access:** Third-party candidates face a significant hurdle in getting on the ballot in all 50 states. Each state has its requirements, often involving collecting thousands of signatures, which can be costly and time-consuming.

- **Media Coverage:** Third-party candidates typically receive less media coverage than their major-party counterparts, making it difficult to reach a broad audience. This lack of exposure can contribute to lower voter awareness and support.

- **Wasted Vote Syndrome:** Many voters are reluctant to support third-party candidates because they believe these candidates have little chance of winning. This phenomenon, known as the "wasted vote" syndrome, discourages people from voting for third-party candidates, even if they align more closely with their views.

The Impact on Electoral Outcomes

In some instances, third-party candidates can have a decisive impact on electoral outcomes, particularly in closely contested races. This influence can manifest in various ways, from drawing votes away from major party candidates to altering the strategies of the major parties.

- **Election Spoilers:** In addition to Ralph Nader in 2000, another notable example of a potential "spoiler" effect was the candidacy of Ross Perot in 1992. While Perot did not win any electoral votes, his strong showing is believed to have split the conservative vote, contributing to Bill Clinton's victory over incumbent President George H.W. Bush.

- **Strategic Shifts:** The presence of a robust third-party candidate can force major parties to adjust their strategies, either by adopting some of the third party's positions or by focusing on different issues to differentiate themselves. This can lead to shifts in the political landscape, even if the third-party candidate does not win.

Ballot Access:

How Third Parties Get on the Ballot and the Challenges They Face

One of the most significant challenges third-party candidates face in U.S. elections is getting on the ballot. The U.S. electoral system is designed to make it difficult for candidates outside the two major parties to secure a spot on the ballot in all 50 states. Understanding the complexities of ballot access is essential to grasping why third-party candidates often struggle to compete equally with Democrats and Republicans.

The Process of Ballot Access

Ballot access laws vary widely from state to state, but generally, third-party candidates must meet specific criteria to appear on the ballot. This process usually involves collecting a certain number of signatures from registered voters, paying filing fees, or meeting other state-specific requirements.

- **Signature Requirements:** Third-party candidates must gather significant signatures in most states to qualify for the ballot. These signatures must come from registered voters who are often required to sign petitions in person. The number of signatures required can be substantial, sometimes reaching tens of thousands, and varies depending on the state and the office being contested.

- **Filing Deadlines:** Each state has deadlines for submitting petitions and other required documentation. Missing these deadlines can result in disqualification, even by a small margin. The deadlines are often set far before the general election, requiring third-party candidates to begin their efforts early.

- **Filing Fees:** In addition to gathering signatures, third-party candidates may be required to pay filing fees to secure a spot on the ballot. These fees can be a financial burden, particularly for smaller parties with limited resources.

The Role of State Laws and Partisan Control

State legislatures, often controlled by the major parties, can set ballot access laws. These laws can be designed to make it particularly difficult for third-party candidates to compete, reinforcing the two-party system's dominance.

- **Ballot Access Laws:** Some states have more restrictive ballot access laws than others, making it easier or harder for third-party candidates to get on the ballot. For example, states like

Georgia and Texas have particularly stringent requirements, while others, like Florida and Ohio, are somewhat more lenient.

- **Partisan Interests:** The major parties have a vested interest in maintaining their dominance, and as a result, they may pass or uphold laws that create high barriers for third-party candidates. These laws can include higher signature thresholds, shorter timeframes for gathering signatures, or stricter verification processes.

- **Legal Challenges:** Third parties often take legal action to challenge restrictive ballot access laws. While some lawsuits have resulted in more lenient requirements, the legal battles can be costly and time-consuming, draining resources from the campaign.

The Impact of Ballot Access on Campaigns

Gaining ballot access is difficult, affecting every aspect of a third-party campaign, from strategy and fundraising to voter outreach and media coverage. These challenges often force third-party candidates to decide where to allocate their limited resources.

- **Resource Allocation:** Third-party campaigns must decide where to focus their efforts. They often concentrate on states with more accessible ballot requirements while forgoing others with more restrictive laws. This can limit their ability to build a national campaign and reduce their visibility to voters nationwide.

- **Campaign Strategy:** The need to secure ballot access can dictate much of a third-party candidate's campaign strategy. Instead of focusing solely on voter outreach and policy promotion, campaigns must devote significant time and resources to navigating the complex web of state ballot access laws.

- **Media Coverage and Perception:** The struggle to achieve ballot access can also affect a candidate's media coverage and public perception. Candidates who fail to get on the ballot in multiple states may be perceived as less viable, leading to a vicious cycle where reduced media attention further diminishes their chances of success.

Success Stories and Persistent Challenges

Despite the obstacles, some third-party candidates have successfully navigated the ballot access process and significantly impacted U.S. elections. However, these successes are the exception rather than the rule, and the challenges remain substantial for most third-party candidates.

- **Ross Perot (1992):** Ross Perot's 1992 independent presidential campaign is one of the recent most successful third-party bids. Thanks to a well-funded campaign and significant grassroots support, Perot got on the ballot in all 50 states and earned nearly 19% of the popular vote.

- **Gary Johnson (2016):** The Libertarian Party's candidate, Gary Johnson, secured ballot access in all 50 states in the 2016 presidential election. Despite this achievement, Johnson faced significant challenges in gaining media attention and voter support, illustrating the ongoing difficulties faced by third-party candidates.

- **Ongoing Barriers:** For most third-party candidates, the challenges of ballot access remain a formidable barrier to entry. The combination of restrictive state laws, partisan interests, and the high cost of mounting legal challenges continues to limit the participation of third-party candidates in U.S. elections.

Historical Influence:

Cases Where Third-Party Candidates Influenced the Outcome of Elections

Throughout U.S. history, third-party candidates have occasionally played a pivotal role in elections, sometimes influencing the outcome in ways that reshaped the political landscape. While third-party candidates rarely win, their presence can draw enough support away from major-party candidates to alter the final results, leading to significant political and electoral consequences. Understanding these historical cases provides insight into third-party movements' potential power and influence in American politics.

The Election of 1912: Theodore Roosevelt and the Progressive Party

The 1912 presidential election is one of the most notable examples of a third-party candidate significantly impacting the outcome. Former

President Theodore Roosevelt, dissatisfied with his successor William Howard Taft's leadership, formed the Progressive Party (also known as the Bull Moose Party) and ran for president against Taft and Democrat Woodrow Wilson.

- **Split the Republican Vote:** Roosevelt's candidacy split the Republican vote, with many progressive Republicans supporting Roosevelt over the incumbent Taft. This division within the Republican base allowed Wilson to secure a decisive victory with 42% of the popular vote, while Roosevelt garnered 27% and Taft only 23%.

- **Impact on the Republican Party:** The 1912 election exposed deep divisions within the Republican Party and marked a significant shift in American politics. The Progressive Party's platform, which included calls for social reforms such as women's suffrage and workers' rights, influenced future Democratic policies and contributed to the realignment of the party system in the years that followed.

The Election of 1992: Ross Perot's Independent Campaign

The 1992 presidential election is another significant case where a third-party candidate played a major role in shaping the outcome. Businessman Ross Perot ran as an independent candidate, focusing on fiscal responsibility, reducing the national debt, and opposing the North American Free Trade Agreement (NAFTA).

- **Perot's Influence:** Perot captured nearly 19% of the popular vote, one of the highest percentages for a third-party candidate in U.S. history. While Perot did not win any electoral votes, his candidacy is believed to have drawn votes away from both major-party candidates, Republican incumbent George H.W. Bush and Democrat Bill Clinton.

- **Impact on the Election Outcome:** Analysts debate the extent of Perot's impact, but many believe that his candidacy contributed to Bush's defeat by splitting the conservative vote. Clinton won the election with 43% of the popular vote, compared to Bush's 37%, mainly benefiting from Perot's siphoning off traditional Republican voters.

The Election of 2000: Ralph Nader and the Green Party

The 2000 presidential election is perhaps the most controversial example of a third-party candidate influencing the outcome. Running as the Green Party candidate, Ralph Nader focused on environmental issues, corporate power, and social justice, appealing to progressive voters dissatisfied with the Democratic Party.

- **Nader's Role in the Election:** Nader received 2.74% of the popular vote nationwide, a seemingly small percentage that had significant implications in key battleground states. In Florida, where the election was ultimately decided, Nader received nearly 100,000 votes—far more than the margin by which Republican George W. Bush defeated Democrat Al Gore.

- **The "Spoiler" Debate:** Many Democrats argued that Nader's candidacy "spoiled" the election by drawing votes away from Gore, particularly in Florida. The close results in Florida led to a contentious recount process ultimately decided by the U.S. Supreme Court in Bush v. Gore, giving Bush the presidency. Nader's candidacy remains a point of debate among political analysts, with some arguing that his presence on the ballot changed the course of history.

The Long-Term Impact of Third-Party Movements

While third-party candidates rarely win elections, their influence extends beyond the immediate electoral outcomes. Third-party movements have historically brought new issues to the forefront of American politics, pushing the major parties to adopt policies they might have otherwise ignored.

- **Policy Adoption:** Many ideas initially championed by third parties have eventually been incorporated into the major parties' platforms. For example, the Populist Party in the late 19th century advocated for reforms such as the direct election of Senators, a graduated income tax, and bank regulation, which the significant parties later adopted.

- **Shaping Political Discourse:** Third-party candidates can shift the political discourse by highlighting issues that resonate with segments of the electorate. Even when they do not win, their influence can be seen in how the major parties adjust their platforms and strategies in response to the concerns raised by third-party movements.

Chapter 9

The Future of Voting in the US

Proposed Reforms:

Ideas for Reforming the Voting Process

As the United States continues to grapple with the challenges of modern elections, various reforms have been proposed to make the voting process more equitable, representative, and efficient. These proposed reforms range from changes to how votes are cast and counted to fundamental shifts in the electoral process. Understanding these potential reforms is crucial for considering the future of voting in the United States.

Ranked-choice voting (RCV)

Ranked-choice voting (RCV) is an electoral system in which voters rank candidates in order of preference rather than just one. This system ensures that the winning candidate has broad support, reducing the impact of "spoiler" candidates and encouraging more positive, issue-focused campaigns.

- **How It Works:** In RCV, voters rank their preferred candidates (e.g., 1st choice, 2nd choice, 3rd choice, etc.). If no candidate receives a majority of first-choice votes, the candidate with the fewest first-choice votes is eliminated, and their votes are redistributed to the voters' next choices. This process continues until a candidate has a majority.

- **Advantages:** RCV can help prevent vote splitting, where similar candidates divide the vote, allowing a less popular candidate to win. It also encourages more candidates to run, as they are less likely to be perceived as "spoilers."

- **Adoption:** RCV has been adopted in several U.S. cities and states, including Maine and New York City, and has been proposed for broader use. Its popularity is growing as more voters and officials see the potential benefits of a more representative electoral system.

The National Popular Vote Interstate Compact (NPVIC) is an agreement among participating states to award their electoral votes to the candidate who wins the national popular vote, regardless of the state's vote outcome. The compact would take effect only when states totaling at least 270 electoral votes—the number needed to win the presidency—join the agreement.

- **How It Works:** Under the NPVIC, states pledge to allocate their electoral votes to the candidate who wins the most votes nationwide. This reform seeks to ensure that the candidate who wins the popular vote becomes president, addressing one of the main criticisms of the Electoral College.

- **Current Status:** As of 2024, 15 states and Washington, D.C., representing 195 electoral votes, have joined the compact. The NPVIC will only take effect if enough states join to reach 270 electoral votes collectively.

- **Debate and Controversy:** Supporters argue that the NPVIC would make every vote count equally, regardless of where it is cast, and eliminate the possibility of a candidate winning the presidency without winning the popular vote. Critics, however, contend that the compact could undermine the federalist principles of the U.S. Constitution and reduce the influence of smaller states.

Expanding Vote-by-Mail and Early Voting

Expanding access to vote-by-mail and early voting has gained traction, particularly during the COVID-19 pandemic. These measures are intended to make voting more accessible and convenient, increasing voter participation.

- **Vote-by-Mail:** Vote-by-mail allows voters to cast their ballots remotely, providing more flexibility and reducing the need for in-person voting on Election Day. States like Oregon and

Washington have successfully implemented all-mail voting systems, leading to high voter turnout and increased convenience for voters.

- **Early Voting:** Early voting allows voters to cast their ballots before Election Day, either by mail or in person. This reduces the pressure on polling places, shortens lines, and provides more opportunities for voters to participate in the election.

- **Security and Participation:** While expanding vote-by-mail and early voting is seen as a way to increase participation, concerns about security and voter fraud have been raised. However, studies have shown that instances of voter fraud in mail-in and early voting are exceedingly rare, and many states have implemented robust security measures to ensure the integrity of the process.

Automatic Voter Registration (AVR)

Automatic Voter Registration (AVR) is a system that automatically registers eligible citizens to vote when they interact with certain government agencies, such as the Department of Motor Vehicles (DMV) unless they opt-out. AVR is designed to simplify the registration process and increase voter participation by making it easier for people to register.

- **How It Works:** When eligible citizens engage with government services, their information is automatically forwarded to election officials, who register them to vote. Individuals can decline registration, but they are added to the voter rolls if they do not.

- **Adoption and Impact:** AVR has been adopted in multiple states, including California, Oregon, and Illinois. It has been credited with significantly increasing voter registration rates, particularly among younger and minority voters, often underrepresented in the electorate.

- **Challenges and Criticisms:** Critics argue that AVR could lead to inaccuracies in voter rolls if not properly managed, potentially registering individuals who are ineligible to vote. However, proponents emphasize that AVR includes safeguards to verify eligibility and greatly enhances democratic participation.

Redistricting Reform

Redistricting reform addresses gerrymandering, where electoral district boundaries are manipulated to favor one party over another. Various proposals seek to make the redistricting process more impartial and transparent.

- **Independent Redistricting Commissions:** A widespread reform is the establishment of independent redistricting commissions. These nonpartisan or bipartisan bodies play a crucial role in drawing electoral district boundaries. The aim is to create fairer districts that accurately reflect the population and prevent partisan gerrymandering. This emphasis on fairness should reassure the audience about the integrity of the process.

- **Public Input and Transparency**: Reforms also call for more significant public input and transparency in redistricting, allowing citizens to review and comment on proposed district maps before they are finalized.

- **Legal Challenges and Resistance**: Redistricting reform often faces legal challenges and political resistance, particularly from those who benefit from the current system. However, successful implementations in states like California and Arizona have demonstrated the potential for creating more equitable electoral maps. This should instill a sense of hope about the future of redistricting reform.

Expanding Access:

Efforts to Make Voting More Accessible to All Citizens

Ensuring that all eligible citizens have the opportunity to participate in elections is a cornerstone of a healthy democracy. Over the years, various efforts have been made to expand access to voting, particularly for historically marginalized groups. These efforts include legal reforms, technological innovations, and grassroots initiatives to overcome barriers that prevent people from exercising their right to vote. Understanding these efforts is essential to comprehending the ongoing challenges and opportunities in making voting more accessible in the United States.

The Importance of Voter Access

Voter access refers to the ease with which eligible citizens can register to vote, cast their ballots, and have their votes counted. Ensuring broad access is crucial for a representative democracy where every citizen's voice can be heard. Barriers to voting, whether legal, logistical, or social, can lead to disenfranchisement, particularly among minority groups, low-income individuals, and people with disabilities.

- **Historical Context:** Historically, various groups in the United States, including African Americans, women, and Native Americans, faced significant barriers to voting. The struggle to secure voting rights for these groups led to crucial legislation, such as the Voting Rights Act of 1965, which aimed to eliminate racial discrimination in voting.

- **Modern Barriers:** Today, barriers to voting still exist, including voter ID laws, restrictions on early voting, and difficulties in accessing polling places. These barriers disproportionately affect marginalized communities, making efforts to expand access all the more critical.

Legal Reforms to Expand Access

Legal reforms have been a primary tool for expanding voter access. These reforms aim to remove barriers to registration, make voting more convenient, and protect the rights of all voters, particularly those in marginalized communities.

- **Voting Rights Act (VRA) of 1965**: The VRA was a landmark law designed to eliminate racial discrimination in voting. It prohibited practices such as literacy tests and poll taxes, which had been used to disenfranchise African American voters. Although recent Supreme Court decisions have weakened parts of the VRA, it remains a foundational piece of legislation for protecting voter rights.

- **Americans with Disabilities Act (ADA)**: The ADA requires that polling places be accessible to individuals with disabilities, ensuring they have the same opportunities to vote as other citizens. This includes providing accessible voting machines and ensuring physical access to polling locations.

- **Restoration of Voting Rights for Felons**: Several states have reformed their laws to restore voting rights to individuals with felony convictions after serving their sentences. These reforms aim to reintegrate formerly incarcerated individuals into civic life and reduce disenfranchisement.

Technological Innovations in Voting Access

Technological advancements have played a crucial role in making voting more accessible. These innovations include online voter registration, voting by mail, and accessible voting machines designed to accommodate disabled voters.

- **Online Voter Registration**: Online voter registration systems allow eligible citizens to register to vote or update their registration information via the Internet. This convenience reduces the barriers associated with traditional paper registration methods and has been adopted by many states to increase voter participation.

- **Accessible Voting Machines**: To accommodate voters with disabilities, accessible voting machines offer features such as audio ballots, tactile buttons, and screen readers. These machines ensure voters with visual, auditory, or physical impairments can cast their ballots independently and privately.

- **Voting by Mail**: Voting by mail has become increasingly popular, particularly during the COVID-19 pandemic. It provides a convenient option for voters who may have difficulty reaching polling places, such as those with mobility issues, older adults, or those living in remote areas. States like Oregon and Washington have implemented all-mail voting systems, showing high voter participation rates.

Grassroots Efforts to Increase Voter Participation

Grassroots organizations are vital in expanding voter access, particularly in communities facing voting barriers. These efforts often involve voter education, registration drives, and mobilization efforts to increase turnout among underrepresented groups.

- **Voter Education Campaigns**: Grassroots organizations often run voter education campaigns to inform citizens about their voting rights, the importance of voting, and the logistics of how to vote. These campaigns are essential in communities with historically low voter turnout.

- **Registration Drives:** Registration drives are a crucial tactic grassroots groups use to ensure that eligible voters are registered and ready to vote. These drives often target young voters, minorities, and low-income individuals who may be less likely to be registered.

- **Get Out The Vote (GOTV) Efforts:** On Election Day, grassroots organizations often engage in GOTV efforts, which include providing transportation to polling places, reminding voters of their polling locations, and offering assistance with absentee ballots. These efforts are crucial for ensuring that registered voters cast their ballots.

Challenges and Future Directions

Despite significant progress, challenges remain in ensuring equal access to voting for all citizens. These challenges include ongoing legal battles over voter ID laws, gerrymandering, and the rollback of voting rights protections. Continued efforts to expand access will be necessary to ensure a fully inclusive and representative democracy.

- **Voter ID Laws:** Voter ID laws, which require voters to present specific forms of identification at the polls, remain contentious. Proponents argue that these laws prevent voter fraud, while opponents claim they disproportionately disenfranchise minority and low-income voters who may lack the required IDs.

- **Gerrymandering:** Manipulating electoral district boundaries to favor a particular party can undermine the principle of equal representation. Reform efforts to create independent redistricting commissions seek to address this issue, but progress has been uneven across the states.

- **Future Reforms:** To further expand voter access, future reforms could include national standards for voter registration and ID requirements, increased funding for accessible voting technologies, and stronger protections against voter suppression tactics.

Technology and Innovation:

The Potential Future Role of Technology in Voting

As technology advances, its potential to reshape the voting process in the United States grows. Digital security, data management, and communication innovations could revolutionize elections, making voting more accessible, efficient, and secure. However, adopting new technologies also brings challenges, including security, privacy, and equity concerns. This section explores the potential future role of technology in voting and the implications for American democracy.

Online Voting

Online voting, or Internet voting, has been explored to increase voter participation by making voting more convenient. The idea is that voters could cast their ballots from any location using a secure online platform, similar to how people currently bank or shop online.

- **Potential Benefits:** Online voting could significantly increase voter turnout by removing barriers such as distance from polling places, long lines, and scheduling conflicts. It could also make voting more accessible for individuals with disabilities or those living abroad, such as military personnel.

- **Challenges:** Despite its potential, online voting faces significant challenges, primarily related to security. A primary concern is ensuring online voting systems are secure against hacking, fraud, and manipulation. Additionally, digital equity issues must be addressed, as not all voters have equal access to reliable internet and technology.

- **Current Use:** While online voting is not yet widely implemented in the United States, some jurisdictions have experimented with it for specific populations, such as military and overseas voters. Estonia is a notable example of a country that has successfully implemented nationwide online voting, offering insights into the possibilities and pitfalls of such a system.

Blockchain Technology

Blockchain technology, best known as the foundation of cryptocurrencies like Bitcoin, is being explored as a possible solution to enhance the security and transparency of voting systems. Blockchain could create a decentralized, tamper-proof ledger of votes, ensuring that each vote is counted accurately and cannot be altered.

- **How It Works:** In a blockchain voting system, each vote would be recorded as a "block" in a digital ledger. This ledger is distributed across multiple nodes (computers) in a network, making it nearly impossible for any single entity to alter the results. Each vote is securely encrypted, and the entire voting process is transparent and auditable.

- **Advantages:** Blockchain's decentralized nature and built-in security features could be an ideal solution for addressing vote tampering and election fraud concerns. It could also provide real-time results and increase voter confidence in the integrity of the electoral process.

- **Challenges:** Blockchain voting is still experimental despite its promise and significant technical and logistical hurdles remain. These include the need for robust cybersecurity measures, the complexity of integrating blockchain with existing voting systems, and the requirement for widespread voter education on how the technology works.

Artificial Intelligence (AI) in Election Management

Artificial Intelligence (AI) can transform various aspects of election management, from voter registration to election-day logistics and post-election analysis. AI can streamline processes, detect irregularities, and improve the overall efficiency of the electoral system.

- **Voter Registration and Outreach:** AI can analyze voter data and identify trends, enabling more targeted voter outreach efforts.

For example, AI could help identify unregistered but eligible voters and automate the registration process, potentially increasing voter participation.

- **Election Security:** AI-powered systems can monitor voting machines and networks in real time for signs of tampering or cyberattacks, allowing quicker responses to potential threats. AI can also detect and combat disinformation campaigns that seek to influence voter behavior.

- **Post-Election Analysis:** After an election, AI can analyze voting patterns, identify anomalies, and provide insights into voter behavior. This information can be used to improve future elections and ensure that the results accurately reflect the people's will.

- **Concerns:** The use of AI in elections raises concerns about data privacy, the potential for algorithmic bias, and the need for transparency in AI decision-making processes. Ensuring that AI systems are designed and implemented to protect voter rights and maintain public trust is crucial.

Mobile Voting

Mobile voting, which allows voters to cast their ballots using smartphones or tablets, is another innovation explored to increase accessibility and participation. Like online voting, mobile voting aims to make the voting process more convenient and flexible.

- **Ease of Access:** Mobile voting could greatly enhance voter access, especially for younger voters who are more comfortable with mobile technology and those in rural or remote areas. It could also facilitate voting for people with disabilities who may find it challenging to use traditional voting methods.

- **Security Concerns:** The security of mobile voting is a significant concern, particularly regarding protecting voters' personal information and the integrity of the vote. Ensuring that mobile voting platforms are secure against hacking and that votes are cast in a private and verifiable manner is critical.

- **Pilot Programs:** Several pilot programs have tested mobile voting in limited contexts, such as local elections or for specific groups like military personnel. These tests have shown promise but highlighted the need for further development and rigorous testing before mobile voting can be widely adopted.

The Role of Social Media and Digital Platforms

Social media and digital platforms play an increasingly important role in elections, from voter education and mobilization to disseminating information (and misinformation). These platforms have the potential to both enhance and complicate the voting process.

- **Voter Education and Engagement:** Social media platforms are powerful tools for voter education and engagement, allowing campaigns, organizations, and election officials to reach large audiences quickly and efficiently. They can also share information about voter registration, polling locations, and election day procedures.

- **Combating Disinformation:** The spread of misinformation and disinformation on social media is a major concern, particularly during elections. Efforts to combat false information include fact-checking partnerships, content moderation, and algorithms designed to identify and limit the spread of misleading content.

- **Digital Campaigning:** Digital platforms have become central to modern political campaigns, allowing candidates to engage with voters directly, raise funds, and organize events. However, using digital platforms also raises issues related to data privacy, targeted advertising, and the potential for foreign interference in elections.

Chapter 9

The Takeaway

The Importance of Participation: Encouraging Readers to Engage in the Voting Process

Voting is not just a right; it is a cornerstone of democracy and one of the most direct ways citizens can influence their government. Voting empowers individuals to have a say in how their society is governed, who represents them, and which policies are enacted. However, voter participation in the United States has often been lower than in other democracies, leading to concerns about the health of the democratic process. This section underscores the importance of participation and encourages readers to vote actively.

The Role of Voting in a Democracy

In a democratic society, voting is the primary means citizens exercise their sovereignty. By voting, individuals contribute to the selection of leaders, the direction of public policy, and the overall governance of the nation. High voter turnout is often seen as a sign of a healthy democracy, where the voices of a broad and diverse electorate are heard.

- **Representation:** Voting ensures that elected officials represent the people's will. When voter turnout is high, it reflects the preferences of a broader cross-section of society, leading to more representative and responsive governance.

- **Accountability:** Through voting, citizens hold their leaders accountable. Regular elections provide an opportunity to reward or punish elected officials based on their performance, ensuring that those in power remain responsive to the needs and desires of their constituents.

- **Legitimacy:** A government's legitimacy largely depends on its citizens' participation in the electoral process. When more people vote, the government that emerges from the election has a stronger mandate to lead, and its decisions are more likely to be accepted by the populace.

Barriers to Voting and How to Overcome Them

Despite its importance, various barriers, including logistical challenges, legal restrictions, and a lack of awareness or motivation, can prevent people from voting. Overcoming these barriers is crucial for ensuring all eligible citizens can participate in the democratic process.

- **Logistical Challenges:** Long lines at polling places, inconvenient voting times, and difficulties getting to polling locations can all discourage people from voting. Solutions include expanding early voting, increasing the number of polling places, and offering vote-by-mail options.

- **Legal Barriers:** Voter ID laws, disenfranchisement of specific populations (such as individuals with felony convictions), and complicated registration processes can also reduce voter participation. Advocating for legal reforms that expand access to voting and simplify the registration process is essential.

- **Motivation and Awareness:** Some may feel their vote does not matter or lack awareness of the issues and candidates. Voter education campaigns, grassroots organizing, and efforts to engage underrepresented communities can help increase voter turnout by making the process more accessible and relevant.

The Impact of Individual Votes

Every vote counts, and individual votes can and do make a difference in elections. While some may feel that a single vote is insignificant, history has shown that many elections—at all levels of government—have been decided by narrow margins. Understanding the power of individual votes is vital to motivating more people to participate.

- **Close Elections:** There are numerous examples of elections decided by just a few votes. For instance, in the 2000 U.S. presidential election, the outcome hinged on a few hundred votes in Florida, highlighting how every vote can have a profound impact.

- **Local and State Elections:** While much attention is given to presidential elections, local and state elections often have even narrower margins and a more direct impact on citizens' daily lives. These elections determine policies on education, public safety, infrastructure, and more, making participation at all levels critical.

- **Collective Impact:** While one vote might seem small, the collective impact of many individuals voting can lead to significant change. When large numbers of people engage in the voting process, it can shift the direction of policy and governance, reflecting the people's valid will.

The Future of Voter Engagement

Increasing voter engagement will be crucial to maintaining a vibrant democracy. As the electorate becomes more diverse and technology evolves, new strategies will be needed to ensure all voices are heard. Encouraging ongoing participation in elections is a crucial part of this effort.

- **Youth Engagement:** Engaging younger voters is particularly important for the future of democracy. Youth often have the lowest turnout rates, yet their participation is crucial for addressing long-term issues such as climate change, education, and economic opportunity.

- **Technological Innovation:** Embracing new technologies, such as mobile voting, online registration, and digital outreach, can help reach voters who might otherwise be disengaged. These tools can make voting more accessible and engaging, particularly for tech-savvy younger generations.

- **Civic Education:** Expanding civic education is essential for fostering a culture of participation. When citizens understand how their government works and how they can influence it, they are more likely to vote. Schools, community organizations, and media campaigns all have roles to play in this effort.

This section emphasizes the critical role of voting in a democracy, explores barriers to participation and how to overcome them, highlights the impact of individual votes, and considers the future of voter engagement. It serves as a call to action, encouraging readers to participate in the electoral process and contribute to the health and vitality of American democracy.

Conclusion

The Ongoing Evolution of Democracy: Reflection on How the Voting Process Continues to Evolve

Democracy is not static; it is a living, evolving system that adapts to new challenges, technologies, and societal changes. The voting process in the United States has undergone significant transformations since its founding and continues to evolve today. This section reflects on the ongoing evolution of democracy and the importance of adapting the voting process to ensure it remains inclusive, fair, and reflective of the people's will.

Historical Changes in Voting

The history of voting in the United States is marked by a series of reforms that have expanded the electorate and made the voting process more accessible. From the abolition of property requirements for voting to the enfranchisement of women and African Americans, the evolution of voting rights reflects the nation's progress toward a more inclusive democracy.

- **Expansion of the Electorate:** Initially, voting was restricted to white male property owners, but over time, the electorate expanded to include all white men, followed by African American men after the Civil War, women after the passage of the 19th Amendment in 1920, and finally, all citizens aged 18 and older with the 26th Amendment in 1971.

- **Civil Rights Movement:** The Civil Rights Movement was a pivotal period in the evolution of voting rights, leading to the passage of the Voting Rights Act of 1965. This landmark legislation sought to eliminate barriers such as literacy tests and poll taxes that had been used to disenfranchise African American voters, particularly in the South.

- **Continued Challenges:** Despite these advances, challenges to voting rights persist, including gerrymandering, voter ID laws, and efforts to roll back protections provided by the Voting Rights Act. These ongoing issues highlight the need for vigilance and continued advocacy to protect and expand voting rights.

The Role of Technology in Shaping the Future of Voting

Technology has already begun to reshape elections, from electronic voting machines to social media for voter outreach. As technology advances, its role in the voting process is likely to grow, presenting opportunities and challenges for the future of democracy.

- **Electronic Voting Systems:** The adoption of electronic voting systems has made the voting process more efficient in many ways, but it has also raised concerns about security, reliability, and accessibility. As these systems evolve, there will be a need to balance convenience with robust security measures.

- **Social Media and Voter Engagement:** Social media platforms have become critical tools for political campaigns, voter mobilization, and information dissemination. However, the spread of misinformation on these platforms also poses significant risks to the integrity of elections. Addressing these challenges will ensure that technology supports rather than undermines democracy.

- **Blockchain and Online Voting:** Emerging technologies like blockchain and online voting offer potential pathways for making voting more secure and accessible. However, widespread adoption of these technologies will require careful consideration of security, privacy, and equity issues.

The Global Context: Lessons from Other Democracies

The United States is not alone in its efforts to adapt and improve its voting process. By looking at how other democracies worldwide handle elections, the U.S. can learn valuable lessons about innovation, inclusivity, and maintaining public trust in the electoral system.

- **Proportional Representation:** Many democracies use proportional representation systems, which differ from the winner-takes-all approach in the U.S. These systems can lead to more diverse political representation and encourage higher voter turnout by ensuring that more voices are represented in government.

- **Compulsory Voting:** Countries like Australia have implemented compulsory voting, which has led to consistently high voter turnout. While compulsory voting may not be feasible or desirable in the U.S., it highlights the importance of creating a culture where voting is both a right and a civic duty.

- **Election Security and Transparency:** Nations like Estonia, which has implemented online voting, provide examples of how technology can be securely integrated into the electoral process. Meanwhile, countries with strong traditions of transparency and public participation in the election process, such as Switzerland, offer models for maintaining public trust in the integrity of elections.

The Importance of Civic Engagement Beyond Voting

While voting is a critical component of democracy, civic engagement extends beyond the ballot box. Active participation in civic life, including involvement in local government, community organizations, and public discourse, is essential for a vibrant democracy.

- **Local Involvement:** Local governments and community organizations often have a more immediate impact on citizens' lives than national politics. Encouraging citizens to get involved in their local communities, whether by attending town meetings, joining civic groups, or participating in local elections, helps strengthen the democratic fabric at the grassroots level.

- **Public Discourse:** A healthy democracy relies on informed and respectful public discourse. Encouraging citizens to discuss important issues, listen to different perspectives, and participate in public debates helps create a more informed electorate and fosters a culture of mutual respect and understanding.

- **Civic Education:** Ensuring citizens, especially young people, are educated about their rights and responsibilities in a democracy is crucial for fostering long-term engagement. Civic education programs in schools and communities can help prepare the next generation of voters and leaders to participate actively in democratic processes.

Looking Forward: The Future of Democracy in the United States

The future of democracy in the United States will depend on the ability of its citizens and institutions to adapt to new challenges and embrace opportunities for reform. While the path forward may be uncertain, the ongoing evolution of the voting process and the broader democratic system offers hope for a more inclusive, fair, and resilient democracy.

- **Adapting to Change:** The U.S. has a long history of adapting its democratic processes to changing social, economic, and technological conditions. Continuing this tradition of adaptation will be essential for addressing the challenges of the 21st century, from technological disruptions to changing demographics.

- **The Role of Citizens:** Ultimately, the strength of American democracy depends on the active participation of its citizens. By staying informed, voting, and engaging in civic life, individuals can help shape the future of their communities and their country.

- **Building a Resilient Democracy:** As the U.S. faces ongoing challenges such as political polarization, threats to election security, and debates over voting rights, building a resilient democracy that can withstand these pressures will be critical. This will require a commitment to democratic principles, a willingness to embrace reform, and a focus on ensuring all citizens have a voice in the electoral process.

This section reflects on the ongoing evolution of democracy in the United States, emphasizing the importance of adapting the voting process to meet new challenges and opportunities. It also highlights the role of civic engagement beyond voting and the need to look to the future with a commitment to strengthening democratic institutions and practices. Would you like to move on to any final touches or additional sections, or is there anything specific you'd like to adjust?

Electoral Votes by State

This appendix provides a comprehensive list of the number of electoral votes allocated to each state in the United States. The allocation is based on the total number of Senators and Representatives each state has in Congress, as determined by the most recent U.S. Census. The number of electoral votes for each state is crucial in determining the outcome of presidential elections, as candidates must secure a majority of the 538 electoral votes to win the presidency.

State	Electoral Votes	State	Electoral Votes
Alabama	9	Maryland	10
Alaska	3	Massachusetts	11
Arizona	11	Michigan	15
Arkansas	6	Minnesota	10
California	54	Mississippi	6
Colorado	10	Missouri	10
Connecticut	7	Montana	4
Delaware	3	Nebraska	5
Florida	30	Nevada	6
Georgia	16	New Hampshire	4
Hawaii	4	New Jersey	14
Idaho	4	New Mexico	5
Illinois	19	New York	28
Indiana	11	North Carolina	16
Iowa	6	North Dakota	3
Kansas	6	Ohio	17
Kentucky	8	Oklahoma	7
Louisiana	8	Oregon	8
Maine	4	Pennsylvania	19

State	Electoral Votes	State	Electoral Votes
Rhode Island	4	Virginia	13
South Carolina	9	Washington	12
South Dakota	3	West Virginia	4
Tennessee	11	Wisconsin	10
Texas	40	Wyoming	3
Utah	6	Washington DC	3
Vermont	3	**Total**	**538**

Primary Process Summary (By State)

This appendix summarizes how each state runs its primary elections, categorizing them into open, closed, semi-closed, and blanket primaries. Understanding these systems is essential for voters, as the rules dictate who can participate in the primary elections and how delegates are allocated to presidential candidates.

State	Primary Type	Notes
Alabama	Open	Any registered voter can participate in any party's primary.
Alaska	Open	Allows participation regardless of party affiliation.
Arizona	Closed	Only registered party members can vote in their party's primary.
Arkansas	Open	Voters choose which party's primary to vote in on Election Day.
California	Semi-Closed	Nonpartisan voters can choose which primary to participate in.
Colorado	Semi-Closed	Unaffiliated voters may choose which party's primary to vote in.
Connecticut	Closed	Voters must be registered with a party to vote in that party's primary.
Delaware	Closed	Only registered party members can participate.
Florida	Closed	Party registration is required to vote in that party's primary.
Georgia	Open	No party registration is required; voters choose on Election Day.
Hawaii	Open	Voters do not register by party and can choose which primary to vote.

State	Primary Type	Notes
Idaho	Closed	Only registered party members can vote in their party's primary.
Illinois	Open	Voters declare party affiliation on Election Day.
Indiana	Open	No party registration is required; voters choose which primary to participate in.
Iowa	Closed	Only party members can vote in their party's primary.
Kansas	Closed	Party affiliation is required to participate in primary voting.
Kentucky	Closed	Voters must be registered with a party to vote in that primary.
Louisiana	Open	Voters do not register by party and can choose in which primary to vote.
Maine	Closed	Only registered party members can participate.
Maryland	Closed	Only party members can vote in their party's primary.
Massachusetts	Semi-Closed	Unenrolled voters can choose which primary to participate in.
Michigan	Open	Voters choose which primary to participate in without party registration.
Minnesota	Open	Any registered voter can participate in any party's primary.
Mississippi	Open	Voters can choose which primary to participate in on Election Day.
Missouri	Open	Voters do not have to declare party affiliation prior to the election.
Montana	Open	Voters choose which party's primary to participate in on Election Day.
Nebraska	Closed	Only registered party members can vote in their party's primary.

State	Primary Type	Notes
Nevada	Closed	Party registration is required to participate.
New Hampshire	Semi-Closed	Independent voters can choose which primary to participate in.
New Jersey	Closed	Voters must be registered with a party to vote in that party's primary.
New Mexico	Closed	Only registered party members can vote.
New York	Closed	Party registration is required for primary voting.
North Carolina	Semi-Closed	Unaffiliated voters may choose which party's primary to vote in.
North Dakota	Open	Voters can participate in any party's primary.
Ohio	Open	Voters choose which primary to participate in on Election Day.
Oklahoma	Closed	Only registered party members can vote in that primary.
Oregon	Closed	Only registered party members can vote in their party's primary.
Pennsylvania	Closed	Only registered party members can vote.
Rhode Island	Semi-Closed	Unaffiliated voters can choose which party's primary to vote in.
South Carolina	Open	No party registration is required; voters choose on Election Day.
South Dakota	Closed	Only registered party members can vote in their party's primary.
Tennessee	Open	Voters can choose which primary to vote in on Election Day.
Texas	Open	Voters do not register by party; they choose which primary to vote in on Election Day.
Utah	Closed	Only registered party members can vote.

State	Primary Type	Notes
Vermont	Open	Voters do not register by party and can choose which primary to vote.
Virginia	Open	No party registration is required; voters choose which primary to vote in on Election Day.
Washington	Top-Two	All candidates appear on the same ballot, and the top two, regardless of party, move to the general election.
West Virginia	Closed	Only registered party members can vote in their party's primary.
Wisconsin	Open	Voters can choose which primary to vote in on Election Day.
Wyoming	Closed	Only registered party members can vote in their party's primary.

Unique State-By-State Election Information

This appendix highlights unique practices, regulations, and historical facts about elections in each state. These features showcase the diversity of electoral practices across the United States and provide insight into how states handle their elections, reflecting regional characteristics and historical contexts.

State	Unique Practices and Facts
Alabama	Alabama requires a runoff election if no candidate receives a majority in the primary, a practice common in Southern states.
Alaska	Alaska has adopted a unique combination of a top-four primary system and ranked-choice voting in the general election.
Arizona	Arizona offers a Permanent Early Voting List, automatically allowing voters to receive a mail-in ballot for every election.
Arkansas	Arkansas is one of the few states with no restrictions on early voting, making it more accessible for voters.
California	California uses a top-two primary system. Regardless of party, all candidates run in the same primary, and the top two advance to the general election.
Colorado	Colorado conducts all elections by mail, sending a ballot to every registered voter, a practice praised for its high turnout.
Connecticut	Connecticut is known for its town meetings, a form of direct democracy that continues to influence local governance.
Delaware	Delaware holds its primary elections on a Thursday, a rare practice compared to other states.

State	Unique Practices and Facts
Florida	Florida is a crucial swing state with many absentee ballots, often delaying the final vote count in close elections.
Georgia	Georgia's requirement for a majority in primaries and general elections frequently leads to runoff elections.
Hawaii	Hawaii conducts its elections primarily by mail, and most voters participate this way, reflecting the state's geographic challenges.
Idaho	Idaho allows voters to register and vote on the same day, facilitating higher voter turnout.
Illinois	Illinois has a "jungle primary" system for special elections, in which all candidates compete on the same ballot regardless of party.
Indiana	Indiana allows voters to change their party affiliation at the primary election without prior registration changes, promoting flexibility in voter choice.
Iowa	Iowa is famous for its first-in-the-nation caucuses, which are significant in the presidential nominating.
Kansas	Kansas was the first state to adopt a strict photo ID requirement for voting, setting a precedent for other states.
Kentucky	Kentucky's strict voter ID law requires voters to show a government-issued photo ID, a practice that has sparked debate.
Louisiana	Louisiana uses a unique "jungle primary" system in which all candidates run in the same primary regardless of party affiliation. The top two advance to a runoff if no one wins a majority.
Maine	Maine is known for being the first state to implement ranked-choice voting in statewide elections, a system that allows voters to rank candidates by preference.
Maryland	Maryland has a long history of early voting, offering extended periods for voters to cast their ballots before Election Day.
Massachusetts	Massachusetts uses a semi-closed primary system where unenrolled voters can choose which party's primary to participate in.

State	Unique Practices and Facts
Michigan	Michigan allows "straight-ticket" voting, where voters can vote for all candidates from a single party with one selection, simplifying the voting process.
Minnesota	Minnesota consistently has one of the highest voter turnout rates in the country, reflecting solid civic engagement.
Mississippi	If no candidate wins a majority in primary elections, Mississippi requires a runoff, often leading to high-stakes contests.
Missouri	Missouri uses paper ballots counted by optical scanners, which provide a paper trail for audits and recounts.
Montana	Montana allows Election Day voter registration, enabling residents to register and vote on the same day.
Nebraska	Nebraska is unique because it allocates its electoral votes by congressional district rather than winner-takes-all.
Nevada	Nevada was the first state to hold an all-mail primary election in 2020 due to the COVID-19 pandemic, a practice that has continued.
New Hampshire	New Hampshire holds the first primary in the U.S. presidential election cycle, giving it outsized influence in the nominating process.
New Jersey	New Jersey has a long history of absentee voting, allowing voters to cast ballots by mail without providing a reason.
New Mexico	New Mexico offers same-day voter registration, allowing voters to register and cast their ballots on Election Day.
New York	New York has a closed primary system but has made efforts to expand early voting and no-excuse absentee voting.
North Carolina	North Carolina has a history of legal battles over voter ID laws, reflecting its contentious political landscape.
North Dakota	North Dakota is the only state without voter registration, allowing residents to vote with proof of residency on Election Day.

State	Unique Practices and Facts
Ohio	Ohio is a crucial swing state and is often seen as a bellwether in presidential elections, accurately predicting the winner in most elections.
Oklahoma	Oklahoma has one of the most restrictive absentee ballot requirements, including notarization or witnessing of ballots.
Oregon	Oregon was the first state to adopt all-mail voting for all elections, a system that has been credited with increasing voter turnout and reducing costs.
Pennsylvania	Pennsylvania's "straight-ticket" voting option was eliminated in 2019, making voters select candidates individually.
Rhode Island	Rhode Island offers a "no excuse" absentee voting system, making it easier for voters to cast their ballots by mail.
South Carolina	South Carolina holds an early presidential primary that often influences candidates' momentum in the nominating process.
South Dakota	South Dakota allows voters to register and vote on Election Day, encouraging higher participation.
Tennessee	Tennessee has a long history of low voter turnout, which has led to ongoing efforts to increase voter engagement.
Texas	Texas has a long early voting period, offering residents ample opportunity to cast their ballots before Election Day.
Utah	Utah has adopted a vote-by-mail system statewide, increasing convenience for voters across the state.
Vermont	Vermont allows convicted felons to vote while they are still in prison, one of only a few states to do so.
Virginia	Virginia has made significant recent strides in expanding voting access, including adopting no-excuse absentee voting and expanding early voting.
Washington	Washington State conducts all elections by mail, which is credited with high voter turnout and efficiency.

State	Unique Practices and Facts
West Virginia	West Virginia allows 17-year-olds to vote in primaries if they will be 18 at the time of the general election, encouraging early civic participation.
Wisconsin	Wisconsin has same-day voter registration, which helps increase voter turnout, particularly among young voters.
Wyoming	Wyoming has the smallest population of any state, which gives it unique political dynamics and a strong tradition of retail politics.
Washington DC	The District of Columbia has non-voting representation in Congress but actively participates in presidential elections with three electoral votes.

Additional Resources
For Research And Study

There are additional resources you can explore to deepen your understanding of the U.S. voting process, electoral systems, and democracy. These resources include books, websites, documentaries, and organizations that provide valuable information and perspectives on elections and civic engagement. This list offers readers a wide range of tools, information, and perspectives to further explore the U.S. voting process, electoral reforms, and the ongoing evolution of American democracy.

Books

1. **"The Right to Vote: The Contested History of Democracy in the United States" by Alexander Keyssar** - This book provides a detailed history of voting rights in the U.S., exploring the struggles and triumphs that have shaped American democracy.

2. **"Democracy in America" by Alexis de Tocqueville**—This is a classic work that examines the political and social systems of the United States, offering insights into the strengths and weaknesses of American democracy.

3. **"The Voting Wars: From Florida 2000 to the Next Election Meltdown" by Richard L. Hasen** - A critical analysis of the controversies and legal battles that have shaped recent U.S. elections, focusing on the risks of future electoral crises.

4. **"Why Americans Don't Vote" by Frances Fox Piven and Richard A. Cloward** - This book explores the reasons behind low voter

turnout in the U.S., discussing structural barriers and social factors that discourage participation.

5. **"Ratfked"** - The True Story Behind the Secret Plan to Steal America's Democracy" by David Daley - A deep dive into the practice of gerrymandering and how it has been used to manipulate electoral outcomes in the U.S.

6. **"Stealing Democracy: The New Politics of Voter Suppression"** **Spencer Overton** - Examines modern voter suppression tactics and their impact on American democracy.

7. **"The Electoral College: A Biography of America's Peculiar Creation Through the Eyes of the People Who Shaped It"** **by George C. Edwards III** - A comprehensive look at the origins, evolution, and controversies surrounding the Electoral College.

8. **"Vote for US: How to Take Back Our Elections and Change the Future of Voting" by Joshua A. Douglas** - This book offers a hopeful perspective on how citizens can work to improve the U.S. electoral system and make voting more accessible and fairer.

Websites

1. **U.S. Election Assistance Commission (EAC)**
   - www.eac.gov
   - The EAC provides resources and information on election administration, including voting systems, accessibility, and voter registration.

2. **National Conference of State Legislatures (NCSL)**
   - www.ncsl.org
   - NCSL offers comprehensive resources on state-level election laws, including voter ID requirements, absentee voting, and redistricting.

3. **League of Women Voters**
   - www.lwv.org

- A nonpartisan organization dedicated to empowering voters and defending democracy through education and advocacy on voting rights and election integrity.

4. **FairVote**
   - www.fairvote.org
   - FairVote advocates for electoral reforms such as ranked-choice voting, proportional representation, and the National Popular Vote Interstate Compact.

5. **Brennan Center for Justice**
   - www.brennancenter.org
   - The Brennan Center provides in-depth research and analysis on issues related to voting rights, election security, and democratic governance.

6. **Verified Voting**
   - www.verifiedvoting.org
   - This organization focuses on the security of voting technology and advocates for transparent and verifiable elections.

7. **Project Vote Smart**
   - www.votesmart.org
   - A resource for voters to find unbiased information on candidates, voting records, and election issues.

8. **National Popular Vote**
   - www.nationalpopularvote.com
   - Information and advocacy for the National Popular Vote Interstate Compact, an effort to ensure the U.S. president is elected by popular vote.

Documentaries

1. **"The Great Hack" (2019)** - This documentary explores the impact of data mining and social media manipulation on elections, focusing on the Cambridge Analytica scandal and its implications for democracy.

2. **"Suppressed: The Fight to Vote"** (2019) - A powerful documentary that examines voter suppression tactics in the 2018 Georgia gubernatorial election and their broader implications for U.S. elections.
3. **"Electoral Dysfunction"** (2012) - Hosted by political humorist Mo Rocca, this documentary explores and compares the U.S. electoral system with other democratic systems worldwide.
4. **"Recount"** (2008) - A dramatization of the legal battles and controversies surrounding the 2000 U.S. presidential election, highlighting the complexities of the Electoral College and recount processes.
5. **"All In: The Fight for Democracy"** (2020) - This documentary, featuring Stacey Abrams, delves into the history of voter suppression in the United States and the ongoing fight for voting rights.
6. **"Slay the Dragon"** (2019) - A film that focuses on gerrymandering and the grassroots efforts to reform the redistricting process in the United States.

Organizations

1. **Rock the Vote**
   - www.rockthevote.org
   - An organization dedicated to engaging and empowering young voters through voter registration, education, and advocacy.
2. **The Voter Participation Center**
   - www.voterparticipation.org
   - Focuses on increasing voter turnout among underrepresented groups, including young people, people of color, and unmarried women.
3. **Common Cause**
   - www.commoncause.org

- o A nonpartisan organization that advocates for government accountability, campaign finance reform, and voting rights.

4. **The Sentencing Project**
   - o www.sentencingproject.org
   - o This organization works to restore voting rights to formerly incarcerated individuals and advocates for criminal justice reform.

5. **The Center for Election Science**
   - o www.electionscience.org
   - o Advocates for adopting better voting methods, such as approval voting, to create fairer and more representative elections.

6. **Vote.org**
   - o www.vote.org
   - o Provides easy access to voter registration, absentee ballot requests, and polling place locators, helping to simplify the voting process for all citizens.

Glossary

This glossary explains critical terms related to U.S. elections and the voting process. It is designed to help you, the reader, better understand the complexities and nuances of the US electoral system.

Absentee Ballot: A convenient and inclusive option for voters who cannot be physically present at their polling place on Election Day. This ballot, often used by military personnel, expatriates, and voters with disabilities or scheduling conflicts, can be submitted by mail.

Ballot Access: The fair and transparent process by which candidates or political parties gain the right to appear on voters' ballots in an election. Ballot access laws, which vary by state, can include requirements such as collecting signatures or paying filing fees.

Ballot Measure: A significant piece of proposed legislation or policy submitted to voters for approval or rejection during an election. These measures, which can be initiatives or referenda, often address specific issues like taxation, education, or social policies, giving voters a direct influence on these matters.

Blanket Primary: A type of primary election in which voters can choose candidates from any party for each office on the ballot without regard to party affiliation. The top candidates from each party then advance to the general election.

Blockchain Voting: A proposed voting system that uses blockchain technology to record votes securely and transparently. This innovative approach is designed to prevent tampering and ensure the integrity of the electoral process, providing voters with a sense of security and confidence.

Caucus: A meeting of party members to select candidates or delegates, discuss policies, and plan campaign strategies. In some states, such as Iowa, caucuses are often held in place of primary elections.

Closed Primary: A type of primary election in which only registered political party members can vote to choose that party's candidates. Voters must declare their party affiliation in advance.

Coattail Effect: A popular candidate at the top of the ticket (e.g. a presidential candidate) helps boost the electoral success of other candidates from the same party down the ballot.

Crossover Voting: When voters participate in the primary election of a party with which they are not affiliated. Crossover voting is possible in open or semi-closed primaries but is generally prohibited in closed primaries.

Dark Money: Political spending by organizations that are not required to disclose donors. Dark money is often used to influence elections without revealing the funding source, leading to concerns about transparency and accountability.

Delegate: An individual chosen or elected to represent a group of people, typically at a party convention where they vote to nominate a candidate for a specific office, such as the presidency.

Disenfranchisement: The denial or limitation of the right to vote, often affecting specific groups such as minorities, felons, or those without proper identification. Disenfranchisement can occur through legal or procedural means.

Early Voting: A process that allows voters to cast their ballots before Election Day. Early voting can occur at designated polling stations or by mail, offering greater flexibility and convenience for voters.

Electioneering: Any activity intended to influence voters' choices in an election, often occurring near polling places. Electioneering laws regulate how close to polling places these activities can take place to prevent undue influence on voters as they cast their ballots.

Electoral College: The body of electors established by the U.S. Constitution to formally elect the president and vice president. Each state has several electoral votes equal to its total representation in Congress, and most states use a winner-takes-all system to allocate these votes.

Electoral Mandate: The authority granted by an enormous electoral victory, generally interpreted as public approval for the winning candidate's proposed policies and agenda.

Electoral Threshold: The minimum percentage of votes a party or candidate must receive to gain representation or to proceed to the next round of voting. This is often used in proportional representation systems to prevent small parties from gaining seats with minimal support.

Electoral Votes: The votes cast by members of the Electoral College. A candidate must receive the most electoral votes (270 out of 538) to win the U.S. presidency.

Exit Poll: A survey conducted with voters immediately after they leave the polling place, asking them how they voted and why. Exit polls are used to predict election outcomes and analyze voter behavior.

Gerrymandering: Manipulating electoral district boundaries to favor a specific political party or group. It often leads to disproportionate representation and is often criticized for undermining the principle of fair elections.

GOTV (Get Out The Vote): A campaign strategy to increase voter turnout in an election. GOTV efforts include contacting potential voters, providing transportation to polling places, and reminding people to vote.

Incumbent: A current officeholder who is seeking re-election. Incumbents often have advantages in elections, such as name recognition, fundraising capabilities, and established political networks.

Incumbency Advantage: Current officeholders' advantages in an election, such as name recognition, more accessible access to campaign finance, and established political connections, can give them an edge over challengers.

Initiative: A process by which citizens can propose a law or constitutional amendment through a petition, which is then submitted to voters for approval or rejection. Initiatives are a form of direct democracy and vary by state.

Lame Duck: A term used to describe an elected official who remains in office after a successor has been elected but before the official's term ends. Lame duck periods often see reduced political influence and activity.

Majority: More than half of the votes cast in an election. In some elections, a candidate must receive the most votes to win, leading to runoff elections if no candidate achieves this threshold.

Mail-In Voting: A method of voting in which ballots are sent to voters by mail, and voters return their completed ballots by mail or drop them off at designated locations. Mail-in voting is often used in states with all-mail elections or for absentee voters.

National Popular Vote Interstate Compact (NPVIC): An agreement among participating states to award their electoral votes to the candidate who wins the national popular vote, regardless of the outcome in their state. The compact will take effect once states with 270 electoral votes join.

Nonpartisan: An election, candidate, or organization that does not formally align with any political party. Nonpartisan elections are expected in local races, such as those for school boards or judgeships.

Open Primary: A type of primary election in which voters are not required to declare party affiliation and can choose to vote in any party's primary. Open primaries allow for greater voter participation across party lines.

Proportional Representation: An electoral system in which parties or candidates receive seats in proportion to the percentage of votes they receive. This system is standard in parliamentary elections but is not widely used in U.S. elections.

Provisional Ballot: A ballot is used when a voter's eligibility is questioned. Provisional ballots are counted once the voter's eligibility is confirmed, ensuring no eligible voter is disenfranchised.

Ranked-Choice Voting (RCV): An electoral system in which voters rank candidates in order of preference. If no candidate receives a majority of first-choice votes, the candidate with the fewest votes is eliminated, and their votes are redistributed until a candidate achieves a majority.

Recall Election: A process that allows voters to remove an elected official from office before the end of their term. Recalls are initiated by petition and result in a special election to determine whether the official should remain in office.

Referendum: A process by which a legislative act is referred to voters for approval or rejection. Referenda are often used for decisions on taxes, bonds, and constitutional amendments.

Redistricting: Redrawing electoral district boundaries to reflect population changes, typically following the U.S. Census. Redistricting can lead to gerrymandering if done for partisan advantage.

Runoff Election: An additional election held when no candidate receives the required majority of votes in the initial election. Runoffs typically occur in primary or nonpartisan elections and are used to ensure a majority winner.

Semi-Closed Primary: A type of primary election in which registered party members can vote only in their party's primary, but unaffiliated voters can choose which party's primary to participate in.

Straight-Ticket Voting: The practice of voting for all candidates from the same political party on a ballot rather than selecting candidates from different parties for different offices.

Superdelegate: A delegate to the Democratic National Convention who is not selected through primary or caucus elections. Superdelegates include party leaders and elected officials who can support any candidate, regardless of primary or caucus outcomes.

Swing State: A state in which no single candidate or party has overwhelming support in securing that state's electoral votes, making it highly competitive and often crucial in determining the outcome of presidential elections.

Undervote: This occurs when a voter chooses not to vote for a particular office or ballot measure, leaving it blank. An undervote may result from deliberate abstention, confusion, or error.

Vote Splitting: This occurs when two or more similar candidates divide the vote among themselves, potentially allowing a less popular candidate to win. It is a common concern in elections with multiple candidates.

Voter ID Laws: Laws that require voters to present specific forms of identification at the polls to vote. Supporters argue these laws prevent voter fraud, while opponents claim they disenfranchise certain voter groups, particularly minorities and low-income individuals.

Voter Roll Purge: Removing ineligible voters from voter registration lists. This can include removing those who have moved, died, or not voted in recent elections. While intended to keep voter rolls accurate, purges can sometimes result in eligible voters being wrongly removed.

Voter Suppression: Any strategy or action to reduce or prevent voter participation among certain groups. Tactics can include strict voter ID laws, reduced polling locations, and purging voter rolls.

Voting Machine: An electronic device that records, counts, and sometimes tallies votes in an election. Voting machines include optical scan machines, direct recording electronic (DRE) machines, and ballot marking devices (BMDs).

Voting Rights Act (VRA) of 1965: This landmark federal legislation outlawed racial discrimination in voting, including practices like literacy tests and poll taxes. The VRA has been instrumental in increasing voter participation among African Americans and other minority groups.

Winner-Takes-All: An electoral system in which the candidate who receives the most votes in a state or district wins all of the electoral votes or seats, as opposed to proportional representation. Most U.S. states use a winner-takes-all system in presidential elections.